Cambridge Elements

Elements in Construction Grammar
edited by
Thomas Hoffmann
Catholic University of Eichstätt-Ingolstadt
Alexander Bergs
Osnabrück University

AF215150

CONSTRUCTIONS, NETWORKS AND LINGUISTIC CHANGE

Graeme Trousdale
The University of Edinburgh

Elizabeth Closs Traugott
Stanford University

CAMBRIDGE
UNIVERSITY PRESS

Shaftesbury Road, Cambridge CB2 8EA, United Kingdom

One Liberty Plaza, 20th Floor, New York, NY 10006, USA

477 Williamstown Road, Port Melbourne, VIC 3207, Australia

314–321, 3rd Floor, Plot 3, Splendor Forum, Jasola District Centre, New Delhi – 110025, India

Cambridge University Press is part of Cambridge University Press & Assessment, a department of the University of Cambridge.

We share the University's mission to contribute to society through the pursuit of education, learning and research at the highest international levels of excellence.

www.cambridge.org
Information on this title: www.cambridge.org/9781009523783

DOI: 10.1017/9781009523776

First published 2026

A catalogue record for this publication is available from the British Library

A Cataloging-in-Publication data record for this Element is available from the Library of Congress

ISBN 978-1-009-52378-3 Hardback
ISBN 978-1-009-52374-5 Paperback
ISSN 2753-2674 (online)
ISSN 2753-2666 (print)

Constructions, Networks and Linguistic Change

Elements in Construction Grammar

DOI: 10.1017/9781009523776
First published online: April 2026

Graeme Trousdale
The University of Edinburgh

Elizabeth Closs Traugott
Stanford University

Author for correspondence: Graeme Trousdale, graeme.trousdale@ed.ac.uk

Abstract: The topic of linguistic networks unites different frameworks in cognitive linguistics. This Element explores two approaches to networks, specifically Construction Grammar of the Goldberg variety and Word Grammar as developed by Hudson, and how they inform work on language change. Both are usage-based theories, but while the basic units of Construction Grammar are conventionalized form-meaning pairings gathered in a construct-i-con, the basic units of Word Grammar are words in dependency and other relations. Construction Grammar allows for schematic, hierarchized abstract generalizations attributable to social groups, whereas Word Grammar focuses on relations at the micro-level and attributable primarily to individuals. Consequences of the differences are discussed with reference to perspectives on the diachronic development of causal connectives in English, especially *because*.

Keywords: Construction Grammar, Word Grammar, networks, language change, causal connectives

ISBNs: 9781009523783 (HB), 9781009523745 (PB), 9781009523776 (OC)
ISSNs: 2753-2674 (online), 2753-2666 (print)

Contents

1 Introduction

One of the aims of cognitive linguistics is to account for the organization of linguistic knowledge (Langacker, 1987, 2008). Among the basic tenets of the approach to cognitive linguistics known as Construction Grammar (CxG), as conceptualized by Goldberg (1995, 2003, 2006, 2019), is that knowledge of language consists of form-function pairings ('constructions'), which are said to be interlinked in a network known as the 'constructicon' (Diessel, 2023), also spelled 'construct-i-con'.[1] The construct-i-con is essentially a metaphor for a sort of enhanced, extended mental lexicon, one which is dynamic and flexible. It admits of connectivities among constructions and structures that are not fully phonologically specified.

Attention to networks unites different frameworks of cognitive linguistics. While this *Element* is in a series which specifically concerns Construction Grammar, what we provide is in fact an exploratory investigation into two approaches to the changing language network that combines concepts from both CxG (see Fried and Nikiforidou (2025); Ungerer and Hartmann (2023)), and Word Grammar (WG; see Gisborne (2011); Hudson (2007)). Word Grammar has many similarities with CxG but conceptualizes constructions and networks rather differently. The model of CxG that we adopt is that of Goldberg because her model is the one that has been most extensively used in historical constructional research. Both Goldbergian CxG and WG are usage-based (see Section 2.3.1). We believe that historical linguistics provides insights into the nature of representations in usage-based linguistic frameworks such as CxG and WG. We also believe that exploring the ways in which the theory of networks in linguistics has developed is important for understanding processes of language change.

Our central goal is to consider what language change tells us about network structure in both CxG and WG. These frameworks offer different perspectives on the structure of language networks: there are areas of overlap, but also areas of considerable difference. By looking at change in both frameworks, we can offer some reflections on the structure of the language network, and the shape and status of constructions.

Given the length limits of this *Elements* series, we can only touch on most of the issues. In keeping with the *Elements'* objective of identifying 'emerging frontier topics', we aim to introduce and explore rather than resolve debates (see also Ungerer and Hartmann (2023)). In what follows, Section 2 outlines

---

[1] Because the format 'construct-i-con', mentioned in Goldberg (2003, p. 219), is useful visually, we use it in the remainder of this *Element*.

some key concepts in work on language as a network and on language change, while Section 3 is devoted to issues concerning constructional approaches to the language network. Section 4 continues discussion of networks, this time from the perspective of WG. Section 5 outlines some issues in language change from a usage-based perspective, with specific reference to network change in CxG and WG. In Section 6, we exemplify several of the issues we have discussed via a qualitative case study of the development of causal connectives in English. Section 7 provides a brief conclusion and consideration of future prospects.

2 Overview

2.1 Introduction

In this section, we introduce key concepts regarding networks (Section 2.2). These will be followed up in Sections 3 and 4. We also discuss aspects of linguistic change (Section 2.3). This will be followed up in Section 5 in preparation for our case study in Section 6.

2.2 Language As a Network

Language has been described as a complex adaptive system (Beckner et al., 2009). Network science (see, e.g. Barabási (2008)) attempts to uncover some of the properties of such complex systems. Researchers in this field aim to examine the structural properties of networks, and the ways in which this structure may be seen to be dynamic. This has implications in many fields. For instance, network science is relevant to the development of transport systems (e.g. urban subterranean railway systems like the London Underground), social networks (e.g. family and friendship bonds which permeate human society, but which vary in terms of particular practices at local levels), and biological systems (e.g. the roles played by different proteins, and interactions between proteins).

Language has both a social and a biological component, and different sub-areas of linguistics have considered the communal and individual properties of language, as well as their interaction. As a result, ideas from network science have been shown to have potential for significant insight into language structure and language change.

Cognitive Linguistics has for many years been concerned with the idea of language as a cognitive network (see, e.g. foundational theoretical works such as Hudson (1984), Langacker (1987), and Goldberg (1995)). More recently, as ideas and practice from data science have become increasingly mainstream in linguistic theorizing, there has been a focus on drawing not just on the theories of network science, but also on some of the methodologies. Barabási (2008, Section 1.4) identifies four aspects of network science methodology.

First, it is interdisciplinary: for instance, ideas from social network theory can influence practice in developing theories of information networks. Second, it is data-driven: the refining of the principles of network science comes about via empirical testing. Third, it is quantitative: much of the work in network science combines insights from mathematics (e.g. graph theory) and (statistical) physics. Fourth, it is computational: this connects with the fact that the approach is data-driven. Particular methods of data mining have been developed as part of an increase in research in network science. These methodological properties have helped to shape new research in usage-based linguistics. Kapatsinski (2018) provides a detailed account of language acquisition and change grounded in associationist learning mechanisms, where the mind is understood as a 'network of simple interconnected representations (nodes)' (Kapatsinski, 2018, p. 12), and where 'a link represents a relationship that a learner keeps track of' (Kapatsinski, 2018, p. 13). Network science has also intersected with other work in historical linguistics (see e.g. Baumann and Sommerer (2018) on asymmetric priming, unidirectionality and population dynamics).

In this *Element*, we take a slightly different approach. We do not adopt a quantitative, computational approach, nor are we concerned with measuring frequency changes, as is common in work on diachronic usage-based linguistics (see further our discussion in Section 5.2.2 below). Our qualitative approach is an attempt to come to a better understanding of the nature and shape of the 'constructional network', by considering data from linguistic change in its discourse context. As noted above in Section 1, we consider two closely related theories of the language network (CxG and WG), to look at what happens in change in terms of properties of nodes and links in the network (including their classification). As a result, our approach is more grounded in traditional methods of historical and cognitive linguistics, while making use of some of the ideas from network science where relevant.

As mentioned in Section 1, one way of thinking about networks is in terms of a 'construct-i-con'. Goldberg (2019, p. 36) refers to it as an ordered set of constructions in a 'complex dynamic network'. Expanding on this concept, Diessel (2019, p. 22) suggests that the network is multidimensional and includes several types of associative relations, which he summarizes as shown in Table 1. These associative relations are elaborated on in Section 4.3.2 below. Our purpose in this *Element* is to explore some properties of language networks from the perspective of diachrony. For example, among questions that a historical perspective on the architecture of the language network raise is the status of the construct-i-con, and the nature of the associative relations that Diessel (2019) proposes.

Table 1 Overview of the various types of relations of the grammar network

Signs as networks	
Symbolic relations	Associations between form and meaning
Sequential relations	Associations between linguistic elements in sequence
Taxonomic relations	Associations between representations at different levels of specificity
Networks of signs	
Lexical relations	Associations between lexemes
Constructional relations	Associations between constructions
Filler-slot relations	Associations between particular items and slots of constructions

Source: Diessel (2019, p. 22)

2.2.1 Networks in CxG

Understanding Goldberg's idea about a construct-i-con as an ordered set of constructions requires an understanding of how she thinks about constructions. Further details about Goldberg's variety of CxG can be found in Section 3, but the following concepts are essential: constructions are form-meaning pairings that function as units or 'signs',[2] and constructions are dynamic and subject to change.

Relations among constructions are thought of in terms of:

(i) partonomies which show the constituents of constructional assemblies
(ii) taxonomies which show set-membership relationships
(iii) links between elements at the same level of abstraction

Such relations among constructions are central to Goldberg's concept of a network. Expanding on this concept, Diessel suggests that this complexity involves network relations within and between constructions, as summarized in Table 1 above. The lower-level structures in a constructional taxonomy are said to inherit properties from higher-level patterns. For instance, expressions such as *at school* and *in hospital* represent particular instances of the [P N]

---

[2] Other approaches to cognitive linguistics such as Cognitive Grammar (e.g. Langacker (1987)) and Fluid Construction Grammar (e.g. Steels (2013)) have different views on the nature (and indeed existence of) linguistic signs compared to those articulated in CxG of the Goldberg variety.

construction (Goldberg, 2013), which has idiosyncracies of form (the prep-osition (P) takes a bare noun as its complement, not a noun phrase) and of meaning (*the doctor is in hospital* suggests the doctor is a patient at the hos-pital, cf. *the doctor is in the hospital*). Nevertheless, the [P N] construction can be said to inherit some properties (such as word order) from the more general [P NP] construction of which it is a particular instance. For further discussion of types of network and their relation to inheritance in CxG, see Sommerer and Van de Velde (2025).

Recent work on the construct-i-con has considered links other than the inher-itance link outlined above (see the discussion in Diessel (2023)). This has led to the idea of the construct-i-con as an associative network, where asso-ciations are 'cognitive links of human memory that have little in common with the inheritance links of classical construction grammar' (Diessel, 2023, p. 14). Associative links are said to help explain processes of entrenchment (see Section 2.3.3) and priming, which are not connected to inheritance phenomena. Both entrenchment and inheritance are factors in the historical development of constructions.

2.2.2 Networks in WG

Networks in WG are of a different kind from those in CxG, though as we will see, both inheritance links and associative links play an important role in both models. One distinction concerns the encoding of grammatical relations. In CxG, constructions are form-meaning pairings, where 'form' comprises syntactic, morphological, and phonological properties. At the syntactic level, constructions are usually understood as involving phrases (consider the differ-ence between the second constituents of the [P N] and [P NP] constructions discussed above). These phrase structures can be abstract and highly under-specified: many variants of CxG refer, for example, to a 'subject-predicate construction' (Croft, 2001; Goldberg, 2013; Michaelis, 2013), which in Eng-lish is said to involve the combination of a Noun Phrase (NP) and Verb Phrase (VP).

By contrast, the syntactic dimension of the language network in WG involves word-to-word dependency relations. There is no constituent structure. Therefore, there is no subject-predicate construction. Instead, the subject of a finite verb is a word that is dependent on the verb, and the relation between the two words is known as the 'subject-of' relation. That is, such network links in WG are syntactically classified.

In WG, the classification of these dependency links also operates in seman-tics. In a sentence such as *Dogs eat meat*, there are not only syntactic relations between *eat* and both *Dogs* and *meat*, but there are also semantic relations between the senses of those words. Thus argument structure is also understood in terms of classified relations (dependencies) in a network, because argument structure and syntax alike involve concepts, and language in WG is a conceptual network. Nodes (such as words and senses) and the links between them are classified and organized in such a way as to be able to represent all aspects of linguistic structure (including phonology), but, as is the case in our treatment of CxG, we focus primarily on syntax and semantics in WG, and the network that relates these two dimensions of linguistic knowledge. Such a network in WG is conceptualized primarily in terms of syntactic dependency relations that are associated (not necessarily one-on-one) with semantic relations (Gisborne, 2008, p. 248), as we will show in Section 4.[3]

2.3 Language Change

The second main topic of this overview is language change. We take a restrictive view of language change as change in the systems of community grammars. At the same time, we acknowledge the importance of ultimately grounding the study of change in wider issues of cultural and social change (see Wolfram, Hudley, and Valdés (2023)).

In the rest of Section 2.3, we introduce some issues concerning approaches to language change that are particularly relevant to the discussion in the remainder of this *Element*: distinctions between innovation and change (Section 2.3.1), analogization and neoanalysis (Section 2.3.2) and conventionalization and entrenchment (Section 2.3.3). Further issues will be discussed in Section 5 below.

2.3.1 Innovation and Change

We begin with the following premise: change starts with innovation. An individual speaker uses an expression in a novel way, or in a way that invites an individual addressee to interpret it in a novel way. Innovations happen frequently during linguistic interactions. Only certain innovations get picked up and transmitted to others in a social network ('conventionalization', see Section 2.3.3 below). It is the latter phenomenon that counts as change (e.g. Croft (2001); Milroy and Milroy (1985); Schmid (2017, 2020); Traugott and Trousdale (2013); Weinreich, Labov, and Herzog (2017)). Any number of 'other speakers' more than two is arbitrary, but in practice we find

---

[3] Given the nature of the examples we focus on, we will have more to say about the treatment of syntax and semantics in WG than about its treatment of morphological complexity. There has, however, been work in WG on languages of a greater morphological complexity than English (see Creider and Hudson (1999) and Gisborne (2017a), for example).

Table 2 Roles of speakers and addressees in language change

Language user activity	Type of newness
A (SP/W) speaks	non-manifest innovative interpretation by B (AD/R)
B (now SP/W) speaks, replicating the innovation	manifest innovation by SP/W B; non-manifest innovative interpretation by AD/R C
B and C (now SP/Ws) speak, replicating the innovation	manifest replicated innovation; beginnings of conventionalization
SP/Ws in a community use the reinterpretation	manifest conventionalization

Source: Based on Traugott (2022, p. 43)

that corpora often show spread to several speakers across a short period of time such as a decade.

Language change is conceptualized here as the conventionalized outcome over time of replicated usage-events: 'instances of a speaker's producing and understanding language' (Kemmer and Barlow, 2000, p. viii).[4] The term 'usage-based' is a shorthand for a complex process initiated by producers of language (speakers, writers, conventionally abbreviated as SP/Ws), and negotiated with interpreters of language (addressees, readers, conventionally abbreviated as AD/Rs).

Whether it is mainly speakers or addressees who initiate change has been debated (e.g. Detges (2023); Detges and Waltereit (2011); Hansen (2012)). In our view, SP/W A may say something and AD/R B may interpret it in an innovative but non-manifest, covert way. If B replicates and transmits the innovation to others (C) they do so in their role as SP/W B, therefore SP/Ws are in our view the main initiators of change. The important point is that initiators of change are typically different SP/Ws and that interaction is foundational to change (Ehmer and Rosemeyer, 2018). This can be modelled as in Table 2 where 'speaks' is a cover term for speaking, writing, or signing.

With the advent of sophisticated data mining tools, there has been much interest in tracking how change is brought about by individuals (e.g. Anthonissen (2021); Anthonissen and Petré (2020); Schmid and Mantlik (2015)), but evidence for how innovations spread to others is hard to

---

[4] For discussion of usage-events from a variety of cognitive perspectives, see e.g. Bybee (2010); Croft (2001); Noël (2007); Schmid (2020).

come by even when investigating contemporary speech (see, however, Smith and Holmes-Elliott (2022) for a study of transmission of a phonological change, replacement of [t] by a glottal stop [ʔ] from pre-school through adolescence in a small fishing town in north-east Scotland). Evidence for how innovations are transmitted is even harder to find in historical work as we have limited access to data regarding interactions between earlier speakers, and preservation of historical texts is spotty (see Section 5.2.1 below). In recognizing change, we pay attention to evidence in corpora that transmission to others has occurred, the last stage in Table 2.

Table 2 refers to 'type of newness'. We understand 'new' to mean 'not manifest earlier in the data'. An addition to the construct-i-con can be said to have occurred if a particular form-meaning combination has not been attested prior to the date in which textual evidence shows a unit to have been conventionalized. Examples from English include a number of clefting devices that focus elements in the clause: *it*-clefts, *wh*-clefts, and *all*-clefts, for example, *It was quantum theory that he wanted to prove*, *What he wanted to prove was quantum theory*, and *All he wanted to prove was quantum theory*. These developed for the most part in the sixteenth century, possibly as new ways to convey information focus after the loss of a 'multifunctional first position' in the clause that could host focused materials as well as unmarked topics (see Los and Komen (2012) on the rise of *it*-clefts). Information structuring was not new, but the constructions used to signal it were new.

Change may involve not only addition, but also loss (Kranich and Breban, 2021). Loss is usually manifest in decreasing frequency of use, and in loss of productivity: a schematic construction ceases to acquire new members, and relics of the original construction are found only in small niches, in different varieties, or sometimes genres. Furthermore, much in language change involves recycling old material and using it in new ways, as was the case with the clefts. One job of the historical linguist is to track the recycling and develop hypotheses about how the changes happened, specifically what discourse context(s), patterns of use, and of linguistic interaction might plausibly have enabled that particular form-meaning pairing to come into being.

2.3.2 Analogization and Neoanalysis

The innovative processes of production and perception that lie behind change include accumulated instances of matching with what interlocutors, including the innovating interlocutor, do. This is analogical processing which may result in analogization, the process by which 'the behaviour of one expression is modelled after the behaviour of another which it resembles'

(De Smet et al. (2018, p. 217), citing Anttila (2003); see also De Smet (2013); Fischer (2007)). With analogization, matches of meaning and form that did not exist before are attested (Traugott and Trousdale, 2013, pp. 37–38.). These processes may lead to weakening of the symbolic link between form and meaning. An example is the development of overlap between attributive determiner genitives and classifying NP modifiers in English (De Smet et al. (2018, p. 215), citing Rosenbach (2007)). Rosenbach shows that, up to the seventeenth century, attributive genitives were largely restricted to animate NPs (*the boy's bike*). By contrast, NP modifiers were largely restricted to inanimate nouns (*a seaport town*). In the eighteenth century, attributive genitives came to be used with collectives (*the court/court's favourite*) and were subsequently extended across the animacy hierarchy. As a result, the distinction between determining and classifying NPs was reduced.

Analogization introduces similar form-meaning pairings into the system. By contrast, 'neoanalysis' (for the term, see Andersen (2001, p. 231, ft. 3)), also known as 'reanalysis', introduces different form-meaning pairings. Langacker (1977, p. 58) identified reanalysis as 'change in the structure of an expression or class of expressions that does not involve any immediate or intrinsic modification of its surface structure'. An example is the neoanalysis of lexical verbs like *will* 'intend' as auxiliaries. The surface form of main verbs and the auxiliaries they were reinterpreted as has remained the same. However, that they were reinterpreted is accessible through changes in distribution and subsequent morphosyntactic changes, such as elliptical use as *'ll*. Univerbation such as *by cause* > *because*, and idiom chunking such as *go great guns*, discussed in Section 4.4, are outcomes of neoanalysis.

2.3.3 Conventionalization and Entrenchment

Schmid's theory of conventionalization and entrenchment (Schmid, 2020) is suggestive for thinking about the construct-i-con from a historical perspective, what is 'in it', and whose knowledge it represents. In Schmid's view and ours, conventionalization is a social phenomenon. It 'is the continual process of establishing and readapting regularities of communicative behaviour among the members of a speech community' (Schmid, 2020, p. 2). This partly ties in with the Labovian idea of grammar as a property of the speech community – that there are subconscious behavioural norms that speakers engage in without realizing they are doing so (Labov, 1972, p. 158). On the other hand, entrenchment 'is the continual reorganization of linguistic knowledge in the minds of speakers, which is driven by repeated usage activities in usage events' (Schmid, 2020, p. 2). It is the result of repeated strengthening of patterns of association represented in memory (Schmid (2017, 2020)). The extent to which the form-meaning pairing is entrenched (for the individual) and conventionalized (for the population) is a matter of degree. Much work in historical linguistics focuses on changes that achieve a high degree of entrenchment and spread, but this is an indication only of how successful a change is, not whether there has or has not been a change.

2.4 Summary

We have briefly introduced networks as conceptualized from the perspectives of CxG and WG. At greater length we have also introduced key notions regarding language change. We now turn to a more detailed look at networks from a constructional point of view.

3 A Constructional Approach to Networks

3.1 Introduction

In this section, we expand on Section 2.2.1 above. We discuss how networks conceived in terms of the architecture of Goldbergian CxG can and have been used to account for linguistic change. We discuss the dynamic construct-i-con (Section 3.2) and then two key features of the network of constructions: centrality and niches, and constructional space (Section 3.3).

3.2 The Dynamic Construct-i-con

Details about Goldberg's variety of CxG can be found in Ungerer and Hartmann (2023) and Hoffmann (2022) and will not be repeated here. But, to ground further discussion, the following tenets are considered foundational for the kind of CxG assumed here:

(i) Constructions are form-meaning pairings that function as units or 'signs'.
(ii) Constructions are dynamic and subject to change.
(iii) A language-user's knowledge of grammar involves a complex, multidimensional network; this is represented in a grammar by an integrated network system known as the construct-i-con.
(iv) A language-user's knowledge of language is usage-based[5]; this means it is based in experience and general cognitive, including social, abilities; it is not innate.

Croft's characterization of a construction below, itself based on Langacker (1987), will serve as a useful basis of our discussion:

---

[5] Not all approaches to CxG are usage-based (e.g. Sign-based Construction Grammar as developed by Sag, Boas, and Kay (2012)).

> Roughly, a construction is an entrenched routine ('unit'), that is generally used in the speech community ('conventional'), and involves a pairing of form and meaning ('symbolic'). (Croft, 2005, p. 274)

While a construction is a unit (a sign) it may be internally complex and can include multi-word constructions such as coordinate clause patterns in addition to prototypical lexical units like *table*. It is also complex internally. Croft (2001, p. 18) specifies components of form as syntactic, morphological, and phonological, and components of meaning as semantic, pragmatic, and discourse functional (e.g. information structuring, such as topic-comment). All internal dimensions of a construction are potentially subject to change. A construction is conventional in the sense that it is shared across individuals in a community, or social network; it is symbolic in that the link is an abstract relationship between form and function that is grounded in language.

Goldberg's most recent characterization of constructions is that they are 'emergent clusters of lossy memory traces that are aligned within our high-(hyper!) dimensional conceptual space on the basis of shared form, function, and conceptual dimensions' (Goldberg, 2019, p. 7). Here 'lossy' suggests that over time, not all data that were originally stored in a construction may be retrievable. Constructions are said to be of various kinds: (i) substantive constructions with a fully-specified phonological form, for example, *bird*; (ii) schematic constructions with abstract variables, for example, SUBJ V OBJ OBJ$_2$ (i.e. the Ditransitive Construction, exemplified by *she gave him a pet bird*); (iii) partially filled constructions that are part substantive, part schematic, for example, V POSS *way* PP (the *Way* Construction, as in *push one's way through the crowd*).

These types of constructions are conceptualized at hierarchically different levels of abstraction or schematicity. How schematic a construction is considered to be can in part be a matter of the linguist's perspective and of the degree of generality at which linguistic items are being considered. However, there is also substantial psycholinguistic evidence that language-users do make generalizations over particular instances (see for instance, Goldberg (2002) and opposing arguments in Perek (2012)). In what follows, we will distinguish between (i) macro-schemas, which are highly abstract; (ii) schemas, which are members of macro-schemas; (iii) constructions, which are members of schemas; (iv) micro-constructions, which are substantive representations of constructions. Despite the differences in terminology, all are form-meaning pairings (constructions), but conceptualized at different levels of generality. This hierarchy is represented in Figure 1 (where 'm-cxn' is short for micro-construction).

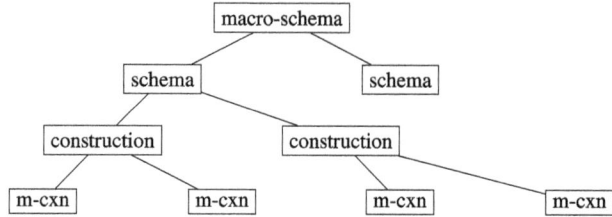

Figure 1 Model of potential levels of constructional abstraction

Cross-cutting the substantive–schematic distinction is a distinction between 'contentful' units and 'procedural' units that has been widely used in recent literature on lexicalization, grammaticalization, and constructionalization. Contentful units are usually semantically referential (e.g. *bird, go, pet*). By contrast, 'procedural expressions' typically guide interpretations in contexts, for example, *so, I promise* (Blakemore (1987) and elsewhere; Hansen (2012, p. 596)).[6]

On empirical and theoretical grounds, especially given the historical evidence (e.g. *lord* and *because* derive from *hlaf weard* 'loaf guardian' and *by cause* 'by cause' respectively), we consider monomorphemic words, whether with contentful or procedural meanings, to be constructions. However, there has been some debate on this topic (see Ungerer and Hartmann (2023, p. 12)).

The hypothesis is that when SP/Ws produce an utterance (a usage-event) they assemble instances of conventionalized constructions that are available in the construct-i-con (Goldberg, 2003). Consider the examples in (1):

(1)   (a)   How old are you?
       (b)   Which armadillo do you prefer?
       (c)   Where did you go?

(1a) can be said to be a particular assembly, at a particular moment in time, of instances of substantive constructions (*how, old, are, you*) with schematic constructions such as Present Tense, Copular, and Interrogative. (1b) similarly involves substantive constructions (including *armadillo* and *prefer*) in combination with schematic constructions, some of which are shared with those used in producing (1a), that is, Present Tense, Interrogative, and some not (e.g. Transitive). (1a) and (1b) illustrate the difference between a pattern that is a routine and one that is not. (1a) is a routine that frequently occurs in replicated contexts, but (1b) is not.

---

[6] A distinction is often made between 'contentful'/'lexical'/'open class' and 'functional/ 'grammatical' items (see e.g. Heine, Claudi, and Hünnemeyer (1991)). Procedurals overlap with the latter, but not all are 'grammatical' in the more limited 'closed class' sense usually referred to in work on grammaticalization: tense, aspect, modality, case.

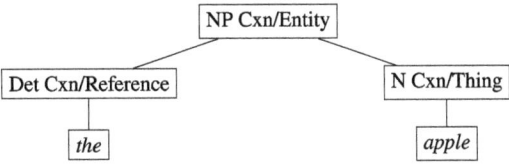

Figure 2 A constructional partonymic network

From its beginnings, CxG focused on conventional idiosyncratic phrasing (see Fillmore, Kay, and O'Connor (1988)). More recently, Hilpert (2014, p. 13) has emphasized the importance of recognizing that knowledge of language is to a considerable extent knowledge of idiomatic and idiosyncratic phrasing. For example, he points out that *How old are you?* in (1a) cannot normally be replaced by *How long ago were you born?* to ask for a person's age. Such idiosyncratic chunks are said to be stored alongside less idiosyncratic partially schematic and schematic constructions such as (1b). But what about (1c)? It is at the very least partially idiosyncratic, since *To what place did you go?* is not the preferred way of asking the question in many communities of speakers. Thus (1c) is not fully compositional, which means that it is not fully understood as the sum of the meaning of its parts. Yet it is clearly not as much of a 'chunk' as (1a) since one can ask *Where in San Francisco did you go?* An important factor is frequency: non-idiosyncratic but frequently occurring expressions have also been considered as constructions (Goldberg, 2006).

To turn now to some representations of constructional assemblies, Figure 2 is a constructional partonymic diagram of the type found in Goldberg (1995) and Croft (2001). The hypothesis is that there is an abstract schema NP consisting of two members at a lower level, a determiner (Det) and a noun (N). Det and N are instantiated by *the* and *apple*, respectively. This representation shows one-to-one pairings of form and meaning. In Figure 2 'Cxn' is short for Construction, and the slash '/' is short for 'is paired with the following semantic property'.

Links between similar constructions at the same level of abstraction are often called 'horizontal' networks. They capture polysemies and various types of alternation. How best to model such relationships has been debated. See Gillmann (2024) for a summary of some approaches to horizontal networks and discussion of how to measure the degree of formal and functional overlap that needs to be assumed.

3.3 Some Key Features of the Network of Constructions in CxG

Among key features of the network of constructions in CxG are centrality and niches (Section 3.3.1) and constructional space (Section 3.3.2).

3.3.1 Centrality and Niches

The construct-i-con conceived as an inventory or repository might suggest a fixed object, but when conceived as a network, it is dynamic and open. Constructions may enter the construct-i-con at the margins and later become more central to it. In the case of the BE *going to* 'future', Hilpert (2008) has shown how in the eighteenth to the mid-nineteenth century the main verbal collocates of BE *going to* 'future' were *say, give, make, tell*, and *marry*. From the mid-nineteenth century to the 1920s, the favored collocates were the most frequent verbs in English, *be, have*, and *do*. He concludes: 'This suggests that the construction has become more widely applicable, and that its meaning has become more general and schematic' (Hilpert, 2008, p. 119). Likewise, before a construction ceases to be a feature of the construct-i-con, it may become more marginal. It may become less entrenched in the individual, less widespread at the population level, and increasingly restricted in terms of potential collocations. The Impersonal construction (e.g. *Me thirsts*) is a good example of this: the only vestige that remains in contemporary English is the (archaic) adverbial *methinks*.

Constructions may not be simply central or marginal. Constructions can be niched, that is, constrained to various contexts, as in the case of futurate presents *going to* and *will* in Canadian English of Quebec City and Montreal. Torres Cacoullos and Walker (2009) explore competing uses of these two auxiliaries as markers of the future in part to determine whether the *going to* 'future' can be said to be ousting *will*. They find that both are robust, but are preferred in different contexts or niches, and are therefore pragmatically not equivalent. The niches for *going to* 'include interrogatives and clauses with complement-taking predicates such as *I think* and *I don't know*. The niche for *will* includes the space of indefinite adverbials [e.g. *soon, some day, never* GT/ECT] and apodoses of *if*-clauses' (Torres Cacoullos and Walker, 2009, p. 347). Even if a construction has lost all its segmental properties, as at the end of Givón's cline 'discourse > syntax > morphology > morphophonemics > zero' (Givón, 1979, p. 209), the formal zero often has functional meaning (see Bybee (1994) on the function of zero in inflectional paradigms). Facts like this require us to think about the network in the construct-i-con not only as dynamic but also as multidimensional.

3.3.2 Constructional Space

The construct-i-con thought of as a 'structured inventory' (Lyngfelt, 2018, p. 1) can also be conceptualized as including networked clusters of constructions from which speakers draw. These clusters of constructions metaphorically exist in a 'constructional space' that is a 'multidimensional space of co-occurring semantic features' (Levshina, Geeraerts, and Speelman, 2013, p. 826). Levshina et al. (2013) investigate the constructional space of analytic causatives in English and Dutch, as in *She made him leave*, where *make* is an analytic causative auxiliary. This relates to Goldberg's notion of 'conceptual space' (Goldberg, 2019, p. 7) in which clusters of formally and functionally similar constructions are organized. It is consistent with an exemplar-based view of constructions such as is outlined by Bybee (2013).

New constructions can be thought of as being adopted into a particular space within this constructional network. As noted in Section 3.3.1 above, some new members may be more marginal than those already available, that is, they may not have all the structural and functional properties associated with the domain when they first appear. Alternatively, over time, they may become marginal members, or cease to be used. New domains in the space can be developed over time, but this is rare. Among them is the English auxiliary domain, which has formal and functional properties that developed construction by construction in the history of English (Warner, 1993). In some cases, new subdomains may develop, for example, the digressive subtype of English Discourse Structuring Markers *by the way* and *by the by* in the EModE period (Traugott, 2022).

We hypothesize that the construct-i-con, understood as a network metaphorically representing our shared knowledge of constructions, does not include every piece of knowledge associated with a construction, such as the largely domain-general knowledge of processing associated with perception and production. A linguist observing the emergence of contextual replications of assemblies that with hindsight might plausibly have led to a particular change may legitimately conclude that it is possible that sets of individual knowledge were modified over time in such a way as eventually to facilitate the reorganization of the network.

3.4 Summary

We have outlined some of the hypothesized characteristics of the network conceptualized in CxG as a construct-i-con. These include constructions at various levels of abstraction and hierarchic relations between them. We now turn to the WG perspective on networks.

4 Words, Constructions and Network Structure

4.1 Introduction

While WG shares much of the same cognitive commitment as CxG, it is different in some important ways. In Section 4.2 we provide an overview of WG, starting with salient similarities and differences between WG and CxG, and then focusing on the architecture of the WG language network. We demonstrate, using a WG framework, a fine-grained account of network structure. This has important repercussions for understanding and modelling how an individual's language network changes as a result of speaker interaction, topics that we explore in Section 5. In Section 4.3, we discuss some key features of the network as it is conceptualized within WG, and in Section 4.4, we show how constructions that have been articulated using constituency structure can be represented in a dependency framework.

4.2 A Basic Overview of WG Compared with CxG

WG belongs to the set of frameworks that fall under the 'cognitive linguistics' umbrella, because it shares the following properties with Cognitive Grammar (Langacker, 1987) and with many of the flavours of CxG (see e.g. Goldberg (2006, pp. 213–226)).

First, language is, like the rest of cognition, a massive network of nodes and their relations. This is the main topic of Section 4.3 below. Second, Hudson emphasizes the fact that both CxG and WG are usage-based, in other words, language is learned as a result of exposure to usage events: 'Knowledge is the residue of countless encounters with specific tokens of language' (Hudson, 2008, p. 261). In both frameworks, more abstract structures (generalizations) are created as inductions across specific usage events. As Hudson points out, this has significant repercussions for how we think about relations between synchrony and diachrony. Instead of idealizing a fixed homogenous system, both WG and CxG see language as 'a constantly growing system of elements with different degrees of "entrenchment" in which synchrony and diachrony meet' (Hudson, 2008, p. 261). Like CxG, WG recognizes that categories have prototype effects and that the representation of any aspect of (linguistic) knowledge may be gradient in terms of the strength of representation. We consider the issues of prototypes and entrenched categories in Section 4.3. Third, in both CxG and WG knowledge of language is a subtype of general knowledge (see Goldberg (1995, p. 5); Hudson (1990, p. 11)). In WG, linguistic knowledge is particular knowledge, both linguistic and cultural, of words and their relations (Hudson, 1984). There is no principled distinction between the grammatical system and the system associated with lexical items. Instead, there is a continuum between lexical items and grammatical 'rules'. As we saw in Section 3.2 above, in CxG these 'rules' are often understood as schemas, that is, highly abstract conventional form-meaning units. In WG, the generalizations apply to either entity-concepts or relation-concepts (see Section 4.3.1). Finally, each form is typically associable with a meaning. Both WG and CxG draw from frame semantics (Fillmore, 1982) in their description of linguistic meaning.

Despite these similarities there are also significant differences, including the following:

(i)   In WG, knowledge of language is reducible to knowledge of words: the research goal of WG is to understand the grammar of words and their relations. Thus the word is the basic unit of analysis in WG. This is fundamentally different from CxG, which takes the construction to be the basic unit of analysis.

(ii) WG is a dependency grammar made up of links, while CxG makes use of networked constituent structures.[7]

(iii) In WG linear order is crucial to form, whereas meaning is organized as an unordered network (Hudson, 2007, p. 285). By contrast, in CxG form and meaning are connected via a symbolic link.

(iv) The focus in WG is on I-language, understood as internal and individual (Hudson, 2007, p. 2), compare Chomsky (1995). Unlike Minimalism, however, as noted above, WG is usage-based and cognitive.

We explore how constructions are to be understood in the WG network in Section 4.4.

4.3 Some Key Features of the Network of Words in WG

Here we outline four features that are important for understanding the architecture of the language of the network from a WG perspective: concepts; nodes and links; prototypes; and entrenchment.

4.3.1 Concepts

Language users have a stock of concepts (Hudson, 2010, p. 9). Concepts are bundles of knowledge associated with both the nodes and the links in cognitive networks. For example, both music and language are cognitive networks, and both involve nodes and links. In the music network, for instance, we have an understanding of nodes (individual notes, and rests) and links ('simultaneous' relations between notes in a chord, and 'sequential' relations between notes in a melody, or chord sequences in a harmonic progression). In the language network, we have an understanding of nodes (words) and links (connections between a word form and a word meaning, as well as dependency

---

[7]   The extent to which construction grammarians engage with the theoretical consequences of suggesting that syntax is based around phrasal constituents is variable.

links between, for example, a finite verb and its subject). A distinction is made between entity concepts (nodes) and relational concepts (links). All entity concepts are learned, as are the vast majority of relational concepts: those that are not learned are known as primitive relations, such as the isA relation (see Hudson (2007, p. 12)).

The isA relation is the means by which we classify tokens of experience, in language and beyond. In the English language, *in* isA Preposition and Preposition isA Word. Inheritance is thus a special primitive kind of relation in WG, and is essential for learning, understood as an act of analysis. Like some variants of CxG, for example, Goldberg (1995, 2006), WG uses default inheritance, such that tokens of experience inherit properties from types, except when overridden. Crucially, the properties which are inherited apply to tokens, and tokens may inherit from multiple sources; isA essentially means 'inherits by default from'. In language, acts of linguistic analysis by hearers involve the processing of a token of experience, either through categorization to an existing type-node, or through the creation of a new node. In WG, the (token) *In* which is the first word of the preceding sentence isA (type) *in*. The reason that this token *In* has the written shape that it does is not simply because it isA *in*, but also because it isA 'first word of a written English sentence'. It is a (learned) convention in a particular culture that in a certain kind of formal writing, the first word of a sentence begins with a capital letter. If a sentence written in such a style begins with a lower case letter, language users do not fail to categorize the word, however. Instead, a default assumption is overridden, and we associate the token to the most likely type following a best-fit principle (see Section 5.4.2).

To illustrate the ideas above, we now consider the representation of the concept 'apple' in WG terms. The bundle of knowledge around that concept, which many people share (i.e. many people know what an apple is), involves a number of other concepts. First, in terms of the sense relations that exist, people know that 'apple' is a fruit, its shape is round, and (prototypically at least) its taste is sweet, and so on. This knowledge is cross-cultural, and independent of the linguistic form used in connection with the sense 'apple'. Indeed, the form used in connection with this sense network varies across cultures. Some people conventionally refer to this bundle of knowledge using the phonetic form [æpl], which has an orthographic form *apple*. These people also know (even if some of this knowledge is only implicit) that *apple* – that is, the word-form – is linked to their concepts 'noun' and 'English' (as opposed to the word-form *Apfel*, which some people know to be linked to the concepts 'noun' and 'German').

Figure 3 illustrates some characteristics of how (linguistic) knowledge is structured in WG. Unless otherwise stated, we will use the orthographic form

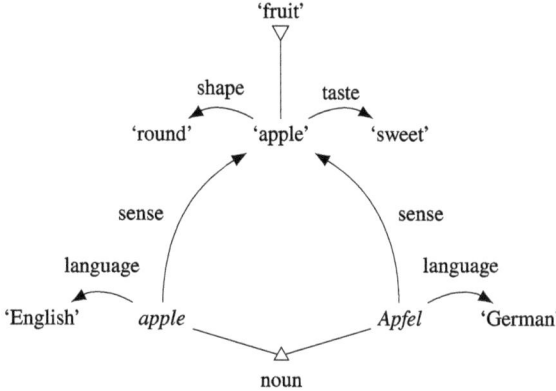

Figure 3 WG model of part of the language network around 'apple'

as a 'cover-all' for any aspect of form. We have not represented in this network the distinctions that are made in WG between fully inflected forms, stems and roots, because we do not have the space to lay out the detailed treatment of morphology in WG. For further discussion on this topic, see Hudson (2007, 2017) and Gisborne (2017a, 2017b). The kinds of representation typical of WG will be elaborated on as further concepts are introduced and refined.

Figure 3 suggests that, in WG, properties of entity-concepts (nodes) are used to both define and distinguish members of categories. Furthermore, these properties are expressed via various kinds of relation-concepts (links). Membership of a category is established by an inheritance relation ('apple' isA 'fruit'; *apple* isA noun). In WG, the inheritance relation is represented by a triangle, the base of which is adjacent to the more general category, while the apex points to the less general type, and ultimately to the token. Because language is a network of nodes and links, it has been impossible to discuss entity-concepts (nodes) without making some reference to relation-concepts (links). Links are so central in WG – and, as we shall see, to processes of language change – that they require some further elaboration.

4.3.2 Relations

There has been considerable interest in recent accounts of (Diachronic) CxG on the relationship between the nodes in the network and the links that connect those nodes (Diessel (2019); Sommerer and Smirnova (2020)) and most especially on the nature of the links. Here we first introduce CxG approaches to the issues, and then WG approaches.

A distinction has sometimes been made in both WG and CxG between vertical and horizontal links (see Ungerer and Hartmann (2023, pp. 33–35) for

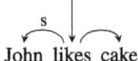

Figure 4 A simple syntactic dependency relation in WG

further discussion). Vertical links are either partonomic or taxonomic, the latter associated with the notion of inheritance at different levels of analysis. Typically, horizontal links are used to account for polysemy relations and variation at the same level of analysis (Van de Velde, 2014). They have been used to promote the idea that understanding associations between linguistic elements is primary. The most substantial focus on the nature of links in CxG is probably Diessel (2019). Diessel proposes that 'various aspects of a speaker's grammatical knowledge are defined by a set of associative connections at two different levels of analysis' (Diessel, 2019, p. 21) – see further Table 1 in Section 2.2.

We now turn to more detail about relations in WG representations. We have addressed the isA relation in Section 3.3.1. Following Hudson (2007, p. 17), we simplify the representation of the fact that relations are indeed concepts by designating each relation as a single arrow with a classified label. Furthermore, we simplify the relationship between argument, value, and function (as these terms, drawn from mathematical concepts, are used in WG) such that the label of the arrow is the function, the concept at the tail of the arrow is the argument and the concept at the head of the arrow is the value. Thus in Figure 4, the function 'subject of' (abbreviated as s) has *likes* as its argument and *John* as its value. A further primitive relation is identity, a 'link between two nodes that are functionally equivalent, so that their properties are interchangeable' (Hudson, 2010, p. 97).[8]

4.3.3 Prototypes

When we think about prototypes, we often think about entities, for example, 'fruit' or 'duck'. But prototype effects are also found in relations such as 'object of'. They play an important role in categorization and in change. There is a vast literature on prototypes in both language and cognition (see Taylor (2003) for an overview). Here we note those aspects of prototype theory that are especially relevant for understanding the language network in WG.

Prototypicality is essentially a feature of categorization and therefore connects closely to the isA relation and default inheritance. The labels given to

---

[8] The quantity relation is the 'relation between a numerical quantity and another entity' (Hudson, 2007, p. 19). We do not explore identity and quantity relations in detail and refer the reader to Hudson (2007, 2010) for more discussion.

categories like 'cat' or *cat* designate the prototype in WG (Hudson, 2010, p. 27): 'cat' is the bundle of meaning properties associated with a typical cat. As a result, any token of experience which we link to the concept 'cat' will be expected to have all the properties of that concept by default (e.g. that the animal in question has whiskers, purrs, has four paws, and likes to be stroked). Notice that some of these prototypical features include quantity relations (four paws), and that the defaults can be overridden (many of us know from bitter experience that not all cats like to be stroked). In language, we see this in operation in many ways. For instance, in English forms of address, the prototypical pattern is for a title to be followed by a family name, not a given name (i.e. *Dr Smith* rather than *Dr Jim*). This pattern can be overridden, such that a person might on occasion be addressed as *Dr Jim*. Over time, it might become conventional to use 'title + given name' in certain discourse contexts (the *Dr Jim* pattern is, e.g., common in UK and US daytime television shows where one of the regular presenters is a medical doctor). As we will see in the following subsection, this idea that atypical tokens may evolve over time to become particular subtypes can be a feature of language change.

4.3.4 Entrenchment

The last issue we address in Section 4.3 is entrenchment. Entrenchment – the idea that a particular representation has unit status often as a consequence of frequency of use (Langacker, 1987) – is important for certain aspects of language change. For instance, it has been suggested that frequently used irregular morphology may be resistant to regularization, while less frequently used forms regularize (compare *drove* with *clomb*, which was historically the past tense form of *climb*) (see Bybee (2010, p. 24) on the 'conserving effect' of high-frequency use). Hudson (2007, p. 53) links the Langackerian notion of entrenchment to the psycholinguistic notion of spreading activation (Anderson, 1983; Collins and Loftus, 1975), a process where by the firing of a specific node (for example, the word *bread*) also activates other nodes, especially those more closely connected to the original node. The connections may be to do with form (e.g. there is a stronger connection between *bread* and *red* than between *bread* and *yellow*, on phonological grounds) or meaning (the connection between *bread* and *butter* is stronger than the connection between *bread* and *table*).

Hudson (2007, p. 53) further suggests that the language network is always in a state of flux: 'activating a node has a more or less long-term effect on it, making it more easily activated on future occasions'. The claim that the network is dynamic is connected to learning in Hudson's (psycho)linguistic model.

This also has connections to innovation and, through replication of the innovation, change.

Finally, Hudson (2007, p. 53) refers to the entrenched outcomes of learning as 'permanent extensions to the network'. He uses 'permanent' to contrast this subset of relatively stable nodes with the temporary ones which are created at every instance of use (every token is a temporary node in the network, as it is the locus of default inheritance). Over time, through entrenchment, 'a token node turns into a type node simply by persisting in memory' (Hudson, 2007, p. 54). This position is aligned with the kind of exemplar-based view of constructions and change espoused by Bybee (2010). From a historical perspective, we would like to know what particular properties of a given usage-event might give rise to some tokens persisting, while others fade away.

Having provided this short account of some of the central issues in the WG approach to networks, we now turn to the topic of the status of constructions in WG.

4.4 Constructions and WG

As noted in Sections 2.2.2, 4.2, and 4.3.2, a difference between WG and CxG is that the former is a dependency theory of syntax, while the latter usually involves constituency structures. This distinction has consequences for how expressions which are understood as constructions in CxG are to be analyzed in WG (Holmes and Hudson, 2006). With this in mind, let us consider CxG and WG representations of ditransitives involving HAND, as in (2):

(2)   She handed me the leaflet.

Figure 5 is an early CxG analysis of (2), from Goldberg (1995, p. 51). We recognize that CxG has developed considerably over the past thirty years, and that representations such as these may not be current. However, we find it helpful to use this analysis as a way of comparing constructional represen tations (which still today refer to phrasal structures) with WG representations

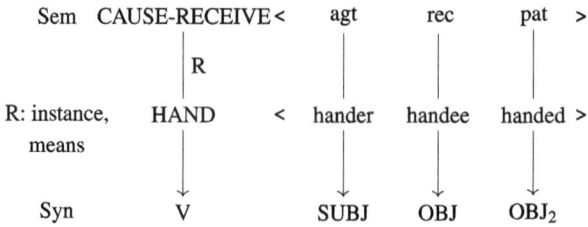

Figure 5 A constructionalist representation of (active) ditransitive HAND

Source: Goldberg (1995, p. 51)

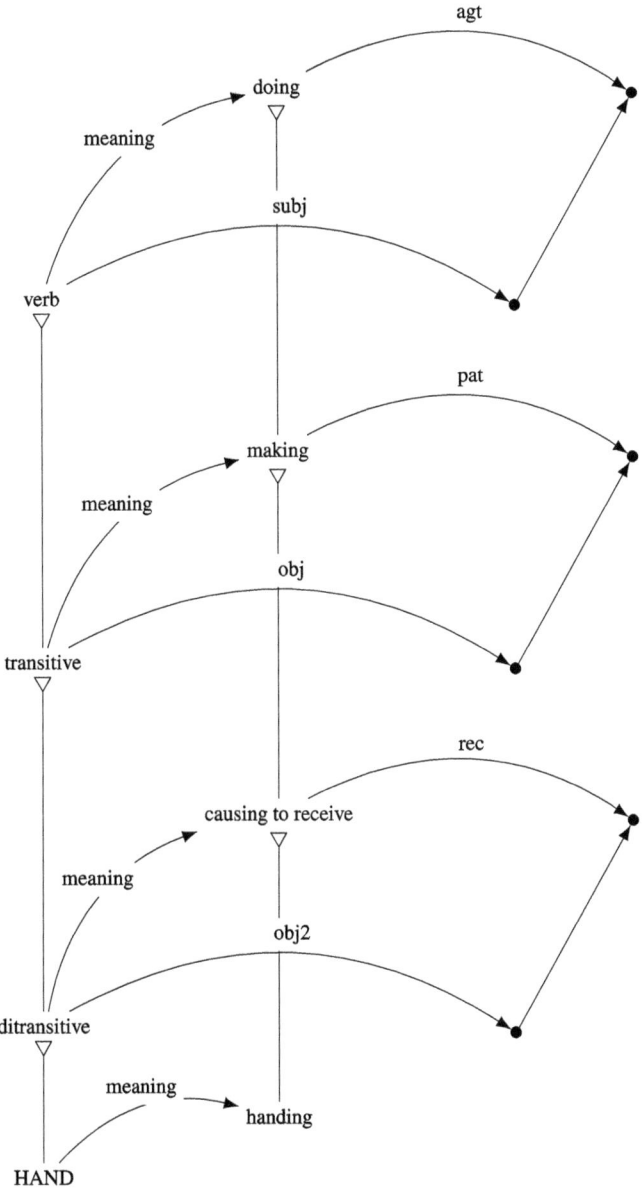

Figure 6 A WG model of ditransitive HAND

Source: Hudson (2007, p. 155)

(which suggest that syntax and semantics involve dependency links). As we show in Figure 6, Hudson (2007) also specifically uses this representation for the purposes of comparison.

In Figure 5, '<' and '>' signal argument structure, Sem is short for 'Semantics', Syn for 'Syntax' and R for 'Relation'. Similarly, agt is short for 'agent', pat for 'patient' and rec for 'recipient', while SUBJ stands for 'subject', OBJ for 'indirect object' and OBJ$_2$ for 'direct object'. Although not represented directly in this argument structure construction, it is fair to say that cognitive CxG (the variant of CxG we are primarily discussing in this *Element*) makes use of phrasal constituents as part of its representation of the form of a construction. For instance, in discussing the 'P N construction', referred to in Section 2.2.1 above, which includes examples like *to bed* and *in hospital*, Goldberg (2013, p. 21) writes that it 'differs from the general PP construction in specifying an N instead of an NP daughter' (see further Goldberg and Jackendoff (2004) on the various phrase structures connected to the English Resultative construction). References to phrasal daughters imply a constituent-based model.

Hudson (2007, p. 154) suggests what Figure 5 would look like if it was directly interpreted in WG terms. There are a number of complex links and redundant phrase level links. His alternative WG analysis of (2) is given in Figure 6, where dots signal underspecified nodes.

Hudson's analysis in Figure 6 is achieved by proposing that 'ditransitive' isA 'transitive' (which isA 'verb'). In other words, inheritance and dependencies together provide a representation which avoids additional (and redundant) phrase level constituents.

Hudson (2007, pp. 119–130) provides a set of arguments why dependency structure (rather than constituent structure) is more consistent with the claim that language is a network. For instance, grammatical relations such as subject and object are categorized relations between words. Specifically, these categorized relations are fundamental in dependency models of language (see Figure 4 above). By contrast, in traditional partonomic, constituency-based grammars, such relations are only implied by the connection between a particular part (e.g. in English, the pre-verbal NP node which is typically the 'subject') and the whole (the 'sentence' node). An alternative way to think of constructions is to think of them as consisting of 'a particular configuration of words related by dependencies defined in terms of more or less specific types of word and dependency' (Hudson, 2007, p. 156).

An important question for dependency models such as WG is how idiomatic structures (from the analysis of which much constructional thinking developed) are to be accounted for. Consider the English idiom *go great guns*, meaning 'to proceed vigorously and typically successfully'. This idiom is an example of a construction in the Goldberg (1995) sense of the word in that it has both formal and functional idiosyncrasies that set it apart from other patterns in the language and cannot be predicted by a language user's knowledge of other constructions of English. It appears to be a 'chunk' of knowledge (Bybee, 2010, p. 7f.) which, while analyzable, is not fully compositional.

Traditionally, WG does not incorporate chunks in its ontology. Instead, the treatment of idioms relies on the notion of sublexemes. Sublexemes have some additional properties which differentiate them from their supertype lexemes. For instance, the lexeme GO in English lacks an object relation, that is, it is intransitive. But in this idiom, that property does not hold for the sublexeme GO$_{/GUNS}$ (i.e. the verb in the idiom *go great guns*).[9] Unlike its parent, GO$_{/GUNS}$ does have an object relation, that is, it is transitive. That object is itself a sublexeme: it is the sublexeme of GUN that must (a) be plural and (b) take GREAT as its dependent (i.e. the sublexeme GUNS$_{/GREAT}$). Notice therefore that the syntax of GO$_{/GUNS}$ is perfectly regular: it is simply the case that unlike GO, GO$_{/GUNS}$ has an object relation, like REPAIR. Unlike REPAIR, however, the object of GO$_{/GUNS}$ has to inherit from GUNS$_{/GREAT}$. Similarly, the association of GO$_{/GUNS}$ with the meaning 'proceed' is also regular (since it could be argued that this is inherited from the lexeme GO in some of its uses (*Go down this street until you come to the traffic light*; *the surprise party went according to plan*). Morphologically, GO$_{/GUNS}$ inherits its properties fully from GO (e.g. the past tense form is suppletive). Indeed, the only atypical aspect of the idiom is the sense of GUNS$_{/GREAT}$, which is 'vigorously and successfully'. What is unusual ('idiomatic') about GUNS$_{/GREAT}$ is the fact that a form which isA Noun has a sense which isA 'manner': a form whose sense isA 'manner' typically isA Adverb.

What then of the notion of chunking? It might seem that chunking is a problem for WG. But chunks are just cognitive routines, and given what we know about spreading activation, we would expect a chunk to be a routine that is entrenched via frequent activation of links between concepts. Indeed, this is probably the best way of thinking about constructions from a WG perspective. In such an account, a construction is a network fragment. Crucially then, the construction is a combination of nodes and links that is activated as a subpart of a more general network.

4.5 Summary

To summarize, WG and CxG are both cognitive grammars. Both are usage-based and posit gradience as a property of both lexical and grammatical categories. They also propose links between form and meaning. But they differ in that WG posits words and dependencies, not constructions and constituent structures, as components in its fundamental architecture. Having outlined

---

[9] We represent sublexemes as X$_{/Y}$, where X inherits from the lexeme, and Y is in a dependency relation with X. We do not specify the word order of X and Y.

some of the key issues in a WG approach to the language network, we now turn to some specific aspects of usage-based approaches to language change.

5 Language Change and Network Structure

5.1 Introduction

As outlined in Section 2.3 above, we take a restrictive view of language change as change in the systems of community grammars. While Section 2.3 was devoted to some general principles of usage-based approaches to language change, the present section highlights two specific issues in preparation for our case study on causal connectives in Section 6 below. First, we consider some issues related to data and methodology (Section 5.2). Second, we discuss constructional and WG approaches to change (Sections 5.3 and 5.4, respectively).

5.2 Some Data and Methodology Issues

Here we consider what historical corpora represent and periodization of the English historical data (Section 5.2.1). We then go on to discuss qualitative and quantitative approaches (Section 5.2.2).

5.2.1 Historical Corpus Data and Periods of English

Historical corpora have been designed for specific purposes. For example, the compilers' aim for the first major, and ground-breaking corpus for the history of English, the Helsinki Corpus (HC), issued in 1991, was 'to produce a fairly loosely structured corpus consisting of both complete short texts and extracts from longer ones', giving 'the date, dialect and genre of the text, the gender, age, and social status of the author, and his or her relationship to the receiver(s) of the text' (Rissanen and Tyrkkö, 2013). HC is intended to be representative of texts from 710–1710 CE that were available at the time of compilation. It is small (1.5. million words) compared to most later corpora and 'represents a very narrow slice of the linguistic reality of the periods covered by its text selection'(Rissanen and Tyrkkö, 2013). Nevertheless, it has been the model for many later historical corpora, including parsed versions of an extended version of the corpus, most of them based on British English.[10] A very different kind of corpus is the large corpus known as *Early English Books Online* (EEBO), which is devoted to texts printed between 1473 and 1700 CE. All the corpora represent written records that have been preserved over the centuries, sometimes by

---

[10] A list of some synchronic and diachronic corpora that are currently widely used for English can be found at https://www.english-corpora.org.

chance, since many records were destroyed (by accidental fire or intentionally). Because they are written, they reflect the usage of literate language-users, and are often texts that were considered worthy of writing down in the first place and then of preservation. This accounts for the high proportion of religious and philosophical texts and histories in the early periods.

Importantly, none of the historical corpora can be considered to represent or be intended to represent directly the minds of speakers/writers in the fifteen hundred year long history of English. Nevertheless, such corpora provide invaluable partial evidence for the history of English (Anthonissen and Petré, 2020; Fitzmaurice and Smith, 2012) without which no fine-grained research could be done. For the cognitive linguist, they can be thought of as windows into the knowledge of a select group of language-users. For the most part they are usually best compared with contemporary written, not conversational texts.

Corpora, and many language histories, tend to be labeled according to large-scale 'macro'-periods. For example, English is divided into the following approximate periods: Old English (OE) 600–1100 CE, Middle English (ME) 1100–1500 CE, Early Modern English (EModE) 1500–1700 CE, Late Modern English (LModE) 1700 to 1970 CE, and Present Day English 1970 CE onwards. These labeling practices are artefacts largely based on external criteria, such as the Norman invasion (1066), the setting up of Caxton's printing press (1476), and British colonial expansion (1700). Although the criteria are non-linguistic, the dates do coincide with certain identifiable increases in frequencies of linguistic shifts, such as the influence of Anglo-Norman after the Norman Conquest, standardization and the development of new genres as a result of the availability of printing (see e.g. Claridge (2012)), and the development of varieties of English around the world (see Schneider (2011); Schreier et al. (2020), who problematize association of varieties such as US English with the date 1700). Periods defined as above provide a framework for conceptualizing large-scale shifts that do not necessarily cohere in obvious ways. Each period can be subdivided, as is done in HC, where data are subdivided into 70 year sub-periods. Conceptual problems that macro-periodization creates are discussed in Curzan (2017), among them encouragement of the mind-set that there is a definable language called English (or French or Latin) and that linguistic change somehow progresses independently of other languages. A major problem is that periodization may imply consistent teleological progression from an ancient state to a middle and final state. However, the trajectory may not be consistent. In the case of English, OE and early ME (up to the 1380s) have much in common with each other in southern varieties, and are relatively distinct from late ME and EModE (Lass, 2000). Another problem is that periods may suggest homogeneity. However, prior to printing in late ME, and the rise of prescriptivism in the eighteenth century, written records reflect local patterns of usage in different communities: largely scriptoria in the OE period, and monasteries in the earlier ME period (Blake, 1992, pp. 9–15). ME was a time when the OE system of morphological inflections broke down and influences of Scandinavian and Norman French contact took hold. Many new resources for expressing old concepts were developed, among them expressions of causal relations, as our case study in Section 6 shows (see also Lenker (2007)).

5.2.2 Qualitative and Quantitative Approaches to Language Change

Both qualitative and quantitative approaches to data feature in usage-based models of language change (see also the discussion in Hilpert (2021, 2024)). While some researchers adopt only a qualitative approach (e.g. Traugott and Trousdale (2013)), others combine both quantitative and qualitative methods (e.g. Budts and Petré (2020)).

Qualitative approaches to historical corpus data tend to focus on contexts and what appear to the researcher to be striking uses that are new, in the sense of being used unambiguously and with relative frequency across different authors and texts. The job of a linguist engaged in diachronic CxG (DCxG) that is qualitative is to track how an addition to the construct-i-con has happened - what discourse context(s), patterns of use, and interactions might plausibly have given rise to that particular form-function pairing coming into being, or emerging. In this approach, if a new construction appears, it is said to do so through a neoanalysis of the link between function and form that is shared among a community of interlocutors. Textual changes are understood to be (at least in part) reflections of mental changes.

In the quantitative approach, on the other hand, constructions are conceptualized as inherently statistical and emergent (for discussion of the distinction between 'emerging' and 'emergent' perspectives, see Auer and Pfänder (2011); Hopper (2011)). They are the corpus equivalent of the kind of incomplete, abstract 'lossy' memory traces that Goldberg (2019) discusses. What frequency changes in corpus data tell the quantitative researcher are the statistical tendencies of particular usage events.

A qualitative approach is consistent with the concept of a construct-i-con because this approach allows for networks of form-function pairings that are relatively stable and are shared by a community of speakers. But a quantitative approach is somewhat inconsistent with the concept of a construct-i-con precisely for that same reason. If a construct-i-con is allowed in a quantitaive approach, it will not, strictly speaking, represent a network shared by a community of speakers, but rather a corpus-derived approximation of a community grammar, in which speakers may show a statistical tendency to align a particular phonetic string with a particular meaning, but where that alignment always has the potential to shift. The more frequently individuals make that alignment, the more strongly entrenched the unit may seem to the analyst, but the unit is always deferred, because it is always being negotiated in interaction.

Qualitative studies can often provide insight with regard to the discourse contexts and rhetorical strategies involved in the development of particular kinds of grammatical change. Complementarily, quantitative studies can give very precise insight into how combinations of particular components of what may later be neoanalyzed as constructions come into being (see discussion of the coming into being of the BE *going to* 'future' in Section 5.3.2 below).

Quantitative accounts can demonstrate in greater detail the gradualness of shifts over time prior to the coming into being of a new construction. They can also give very fine-grained insight into changes over time in collocational preferences after a new construction has appeared (see e.g. Hilpert (2008, 2021)). Furthermore, in the quantitative approach, constructions are conceptualized as inherently statistical. Hilpert (2008, 2013, 2021) has developed sophisticated quantitative methods for analyzing mainly what we call constructional shifts post-constructionalization (see Section 5.3.1 immediately below). In this work, which is highly granular, less attention is paid to context outside the immediate clause. What the corpus data tell us are the statistical tendencies of particular usage events.

Qualitative accounts are similarly concerned with the gradual spread of change, while also recognizing that various neoanalyses and analogizations occur at different linguistic levels instantaneously in the minds of individual speakers. In the qualitative approach, constructions are not typically conceptualized as inherently statistical, beyond recognizing that new constructions may be weakly entrenched, and that increased entrenchment is a product of frequency. The aim in the qualitative approach is to examine historical evidence as to when speakers appeared to have reached a consensus that a particular meaning can be coded using a specific form, where that particular coding was not attested in earlier periods.

Diachronic work in WG has also involved both quantitative and qualitative methods, though with a strong tendency towards the latter. Hudson (1997a,b) outlines the debate between a Principles and Parameters account of the development of auxiliary *do* in English (e.g. Kroch (1989)) and models based on prototype categorization (including Warner (1993)), arguing that the quantitative data better support the prototype view. Gisborne (2011) considers a change related to the development of English auxiliary *do*, namely the development of the English modals, along with the loss of the English impersonal construction.

This research is very close in spirit to some of the ideas outlined in the present work, in that it focuses on how we are to understand recurrent pathways of change (such as those proposed by work in grammaticalization studies) in terms of the reconfiguration of network links. Similarly, Gisborne (2017a) is a qualitative study concerned with understanding the role of inheritance in cases of grammaticalization, such as the early stages of the development of the Romance future, as well as with later grammaticalization in the shift from clitic to affix. We return to these issues in Section 5.4 below.

5.3 Constructional Approaches to Language Change

In this subsection, we turn to constructional approaches to language change. We revisit a concept that has been much debated in diachronic approaches to CxG, namely constructionalization, and also look at shifts in contextual use (Section 5.3.1). In Section 5.3.2, we address a question that is central to critiques of the notion constructionalization: how do we know when a new construction has arisen?

5.3.1 Constructionalization and Constructional Shifts

Studies of the historical development of constructions are collectively known as studies in DCxG, see Barðdal, Smirnova, Sommerer, & Gildea (2015), Gildea and Barðdal (2023). One disputed dimension of DCxG is constructionalization, a hypothesis about how constructions come into being (e.g. Traugott and Trousdale (2013)). Our original characterization in Traugott and Trousdale (2013, p. 22) was, in part, 'Constructionalization is the creation of form$_{new}$-meaning$_{new}$ (combinations of) signs'. This characterization has been the subject of significant criticism in the literature (e.g. Börjars, Vincent, and Walkden (2015), Flach (2020), and Smirnova and Sommerer (2020)).

Flach (2020, p. 48) argues that the term 'constructionalization' is 'ambiguous between a "process" and a "point" reading: it refers simultaneously to constructional changes surrounding the new node and the new node itself'. We suggest that one way to address the problem is to be clear in distinguishing innovation and change (see Section 2.3.1). Innovation, understood as an individual's creation of a new symbolic link between form and function, is a point. It is a new cognitive representation in an individual and is instantaneous. But without two subsequent processes, there would be no change. One process is cognitive and individual (entrenchment) and the other is social and communicative (conventionalization). A construction is a conventional symbolic unit. Conventionalization of a form-function pair with a symbolic link is the (social) outcome of a community or network of language users adopting the innovation, while unit status of a form-function pair is the (cognitive) outcome of increased frequency of use. The more this unit spreads, the more embedded it becomes in the construct-i-con. Both the increase in 'unit-like' status, and the social spread of the unit, are gradual processes. The combination of the innovation, its cognitive entrenchments and its social conventionalization results in a new construction being added to the construct-i-con. Given this analysis, our current characterization of constructionalization is:

> Constructionalization is the development of a new symbolic link between a form and a function which has been replicated across a network of language users and which results in an addition to the construct-i-con.

If constructionalization occurs, neoanalysis of the link between function and form is shared among a community of interlocutors. Some characteristics of new constructions include that (i) their meaning is independent of the contexts which enabled them; (ii) they may become more entrenched (i.e. accessed as a unit) at the level of the individual speaker and more widespread at the level of the social network, or population; and (iii) they may be non-compositional (i.e. the meanings cannot be entirely determined from the parts).

An example which illustrates these three characteristics is the development of adverbial *by the way* as a Discourse Structuring Marker (Traugott, 2022, pp. 139–154). While *by the way* originally instantiated the concepts of location at or movement along a literal path, it came to be used as a rhetorical device concerning the progression of (and digression from) an argument. Thus (i) the meaning has become emancipated from the enabling context, because there has been extension from verbs of location/direction to verbs of saying/locution; (ii) the form has become entrenched because the sequence when it functions as a discourse marker is not interruptable (*by the long way); and (iii) the expression is non-compositional.

Not all change involves the creation of a symbolic unit. The term 'constructional changes' that Traugott and Trousdale (2013, p. 26) used for such phenomena led to difficulties in distinguishing them from constructionalizations. A new characterization of what we now call 'constructional shifts' is (see further Traugott (2022, p. 51)):

> Constructional shifts are shifts in contextual uses prior to and following constructionalization. They include but are not limited to: replication of assemblies, frequency variation, degrees of association with specific genres and with the social characteristics of language users. They do not result in additions to the construct-i-con.

Pre-constructionalization, constructional shifts tend to be changes in the frequency with which a certain construction is combined or assembled with another construction (see Petré (2019)). Replication of assemblies is a characteristic of production. It is evidenced by shifts in the frequency with which particular assemblies occur in the data. Interpretation of implicatures arising from the replications is a characteristic of perception. It is evidenced by increase in AD/Rs' difficulty in interpreting a usage in its original sense.

Post-constructionalization, constructional shifts tend to be host-class expansions, extensions of the collocational range of a particular item. For example, the English future BE *going to*, during the Modern period, came to collocate with a stative verb such as *be*, in addition to an action verb such as *make*. They are discussed in Barðdal (2008) and Traugott and Trousdale (2013) under the term 'productivity'. The new construction is extensible: it can be used in expanded contexts (this is called 'syntagmatic' extension) and, if it is schematic, the set of which the new construction is a part may be expanded by the addition of more constructions to the category (this is called 'onomasiological' extension). Such expansions have frequency effects (De Smet (2012); Hilpert (2008, 2013)). In some cases the host-class expansions may result in the development of schemas and organizational shifts within a network (see Torrent (2015)).

Whether occurring pre- or post-constructionalization, constructional shifts are instantaneous in individual processing, but gradual to the extent that they are replicated and diffused in often barely perceptible steps (the spread of attributive NP modifiers mentioned above in Section 2.3.2 under analogization is an example). Shifts before and after constructionalization may be almost imperceptible or 'sneaky' (De Smet (2012, p. 608), on actualization post-constructionalization). A good example of the sneakiness of post-constructionalization changes is the semantic-pragmatic development of *silly* from ME 'innocent' (originally 'blessed') to EModE 'foolish' as described in the OED (see Hollmann (2009)).

5.3.2 How Do We Know When a New Construction Has Arisen?

Much as one might wish to be able to identify a 'precise . . . starting point for a change' (Börjars et al., 2015, p. 372), or a precise point for its result in a new construction, the nature of the data is such that such precise dates of change are largely unknowable for any unit of language. Corpora and other data bases can only be representative of the texts of a period (see Section 5.2.1 above). They cannot capture every utterance by every SP/W.

We can, however, identify approximate dates, because uses of the new construction that are unambiguous and independent of the enabling contexts start to be attested in corpora and to be used by two or more different writers possibly within the period of a generation (roughly 25 years). Researchers tend to note increased frequency at such periods. Conventionalization attested by use across several different speakers results in greater frequency than the sporadic pre-constructionalization examples that sometimes appear, but the frequency with which new constructions are attested is often quite low.

By hypothesis, when new constructions arise there is fading of the biographical local contexts of use that produced the innovations (speakers, place of utterance etc.). This is because constructionalization is the development of a shared abstraction over tokens. Is there also erasure of the local co-texts? Only to the extent that the new construction can be used independently of them, but typically co-texts that were historically enabling continue to be used. They no longer enable the development of the new construction. Rather, they now reinforce it and may, post-constructionalization, contribute to its alignment to the schema of which it has become a member.

Consider, for example, the development of BE *going to* 'future'. This is one of the most cited constructional changes in the history of English. In the early 1700s it was constructionalized and added to the construct-i-con. There were earlier deictic future markers such as *will* and *shall*, and components of BE *going to* V are attested from the 1500s, specifically BE + V-*ing* and *go to* V 'motion with a purpose', but the sequence BE *going to* unambiguously cueing 'future' because it occurs in contexts without an animate subject does not occur prior to the 1700s. Around this period a half-dozen or so examples appear in different texts found in the corpora. An early example is (3):

(3)　　. . . told him there was going to be an Inquisition made in some accounts
　　　　'. . . told him an inquiry was going to be made into some accounts'
　　　　(1701 Anonymous [Petré (2019, p. 168)])

How did this new construction come into being? The standard view has been that there was an earlier BE *going to* V 'motion-with-a-purpose' construction. However, Petré (2019) hypothesizes that there was no such 'motion' construction in EModE because the sequence is too compositional to be a construction. Rather, there were three separate constructions as in (4) from about 1500 on that were assembled in sequence with increasing frequency:

(4)　　(a)　[[BE + V$_{ing}$] ↔ ['ongoing activity']]
　　　　(b)　[[GO] ↔ ['go']]
　　　　(c)　[[*to* + INF] ↔ ['intended activity']]

Budts and Petré (2020) show how particular assemblies of the three constructions in (4) in topicalized and passive sentences increased from the 1620s and

1640s respectively, compared to use in non-topicalized and active sentences. In (5a) *Lady Mary* is topicalized in the relative clause (*whom*), and motion is deprofiled. In (5b) *is going to be taken away from me* is a passive expression that deprofiles the agent, which must be pragmatically inferred. In both cases motion with a purpose cannot be ruled out, despite the deprofiling of a semantic feature.

(5)　　(a)　Lady Mary of Burgundy [. . .], whom he was going to marrie when death [. . .] preuented him (1585 [Budts and Petré (2020, p. 326)])
　　　　(b)　you see that my Magazin ('storage place for gun cartridges') is going to be taken from me (1642 [Budts and Petré (2020, p. 330)]).

These are constructional shifts which enabled the constructionalization of BE *going to* 'future' at the beginning of the eighteenth century. As mentioned above in Section 5.3.1, post-constructionalization of BE *going to* 'future' there was host-class expansion of the verbs with which the construction collocates. Each new collocation that is found to be replicated in the data is a constructional shift.

5.4 WG Approaches to Language Change

In Section 4.4, we outlined similarities and differences between WG and CxG. In this section, we consider how the WG framework may be applied to instances of language change, and make comparisons with current themes in diachronic approaches to CxG.

In the first three subsections, we provide an overview of WG and change. We begin by summarizing some previous accounts of change in WG (Section 5.4.1). We then identify a key issue in the framework that is relevant to the study of innovation and change: how nodes and links are built (Section 5.4.2). Finally, we outline implications of WG for network theories of change (Section 5.4.3).

5.4.1 Some Previous Accounts of Diachronic Variation in WG

The majority of work in WG has been synchronic in its focus. However, a few studies have addressed patterns of diachronic variation and bring out relevant issues for points of comparison with CxG. We provide a summary of four such studies here.

Hudson (1997a, 1997b) discusses the development of *do*-periphrasis in English, comparing the formal competition model of syntactic change in Kroch (1989) with the accounts of Denison (1993) and especially Warner (1993). Warner focuses on the gradual divergence of two subcategories of English verb:

full verb and auxiliary verb. Our attention here is on Hudson's claim that linguistic change involves change in network structure. Specifically, drawing on the findings of Warner (1993), Hudson (1997a) brings together the changes affecting some of the modals (e.g. loss of non-finite forms of *may* and *can*) with developments affecting auxiliary *do* at approximately the same period (e.g. near obligatory appearance of auxiliary *do* in questions). The essence of the argument is that what changes in the history of English are the grammatical properties of the two subclasses of verb, such that the category 'auxiliary verb' becomes more sharply distinct from that of the category 'full verb'.[11] While there were a few features to distinguish auxiliaries from full verbs in Old English – Warner (1993) identifies properties such as negative forms with *n-* such as *nylle* 'don't want' – there are more features in the Modern period (such as the ability to be directly negated with *n't*, appearance in tag questions and the taking of a non-finite verb as a dependent). The network element of this account lies in the treatment of word classes as prototypes, 'mental categories which link characteristics in bundles' (Hudson, 1997a, pp. 104–105). Specifically, membership of either category does not change extensively throughout the history of English (see Hudson (1997a, p. 103)); what changes are the properties of each subnetwork of 'verb' (i.e. auxiliary vs. full).

Gisborne (2011) provides a more extensive account of network change. This account, like Hudson (1997a, 1997b), looks at English auxiliation, and is supplemented by a discussion of the loss of an argument structure construction in English, the impersonal. For reasons of space, we discuss only the auxiliation study here. Gisborne's article is especially important for the ideas expounded in this *Element* because it directly addresses the relationship between WG, CxG and diachrony. In particular, Gisborne (2011, p. 156) suggests that WG is a phrase-free CxG. In his view, both the nodes and the links (the lexical items and the dependencies) are constructions. We would like to refine this further to say that it is the particular arrangement of nodes and links (a subnetwork) that most closely resembles the constructions in CxG. Gisborne (2011, pp. 158–159) observes that a central difference between CxG and WG concerns the nature of the network: for CxG, the network must involve part-whole relations (in order to motivate phrase structure) while for WG, the network for most of syntax consists only of inheritance (isA) links and associative relations. Crucially, associative relations work across the phrasal levels of CxG: the link between the form *book* and the meaning 'book' is an associative relation

---

[11] A non-linguistic parallel is the distinction between 'jeans' and 'trousers'. Historically, 'jeans' were a subtype of 'trousers' but have become so distinctive that it is now possible to ask *Will you be wearing jeans or trousers?*

(classified as 'sense of'), just as the link between the head *jump* and the dependent *Kangaroos* in the expression *Kangaroos jump* is an associative relation (classified as 'subject of'). This is important for our understanding of both the extent of and connections between linguistic changes in WG: change can only refer to the creation, loss, or variation in entrenchment of nodes and links. Changes are connected because different areas of language are linked, with variation in one subarea capable of inducing variation in another.

Gisborne's analysis of the development of English auxiliaries draws on the following set of claims:

(i)   In terms of syntactic structure, contemporary modals, like other raising verbs such as *seem*, take a non-finite dependent. That associative relation is classified as 'xcomp' (denoting a predicative complement). Both the finite verb and the non-finite form have a pre-dependent, which is the value of the 'subject of' relation.

(ii) While various verbs may form part of the same syntactic xcomp configuration, the associative links to and between the semantic configurations vary in some significant ways. For instance, *seem* does not assign an argument role to the subject, while *try* does. Specifically, *try* assigns the role of Agent to the subject argument. Similarly, in terms of event structure, the combination of *will* and a full verb 'denotes a single event' (Gisborne, 2011, p. 167), while that of *intend* and its xcomp denotes two events (Gisborne, 2011, pp. 171–172, especially figures 4 and 5). Here we see a further parallel between WG and CxG. In both frameworks, semantic polysemies can be connected to properties of the lexical semantics of particular verbs in argument structure constructions (compare intended transfer with *bake* and denial of transfer with *refuse* in the Ditransitive Construction).

(iii) Thus, the auxiliation process involves changes in both form and meaning, and not just at the level of a change to the category of a single lexical item. As Gisborne (2011, p. 172) observes, 'it cannot just be the case that the word WILL underwent grammaticalization: the whole construction had to emerge as well, because of the structural difference between having a relationship between events, and one where the event is shared between the xcomp's head and the xcomp'. Such a position is similar to the one proposed, within CxG terms, by Traugott and Trousdale (2013), whose view of constructionalization involved the creation of a conventional form$_{new}$-meaning$_{new}$ unit. As we will argue in the rest of this Section, the WG position allows for a clear articulation of some aspects of micro-changes in the network.

In more recent work, Gisborne (2017a) addresses more highly grammaticalized patterns, such as the (morphological) Romance future markers. However, he also refers to the earlier stages of this grammaticalization trajectory, by looking at the earlier history of Latin HABERE. In order to explain the primary grammaticalization stage, Gisborne (2017a) draws on the notion of the sublexeme (discussed in Section 4.4 above). In the case of the source of the Romance future, the sublexeme $\text{HABERE}_{/\text{INF}}$ [12] inherits certain properties from the lexeme HABERE (e.g. its orthography and phonology), but it also has associative links that are distinct from HABERE. For instance, $\text{HABERE}_{/\text{INF}}$ forms an xcomp relation with a preceding infinitive verb, and its meaning relation has a value 'future'. Subsequent morphophonlogical changes result in the creation of clitics and then affixes (for further details, see Gisborne (2017a, pp. 165–174)).

Finally, Trousdale (2025) considers diachronic development in word-formation patterns in the history of English from a WG position. Specifically, the research looks at the development of two affixes, *-ster* and *-ish* as in *fraudster* and *blackish* respectively. For present purposes, the key issues that Trousdale (2025) addresses concern the extent of shift in a network when new constructions emerge, and the ways in which such shifts should be classified. In the WG analysis provided, Trousdale shows that the new word-formation constructions (again, understood as a combination of nodes and links) involve very small-scale shifts. For *-ster*, new constructions arise from 'a reassociation of *-ster* attaching to bases which isA different lexical (sub)categories' (Trousdale, 2025, p. 122). There are small sense developments which run in parallel with the shifts to the associations with different categories of base, but these are very local, and essentially involve the creation of new associative links in both form and meaning. For example, there is a shift from OE *demster* 'judge', where the affix attaches to a verbal base, to ModE *gangster*, with a nominal base. With *-ish*, the shifts appear more substantial (since the dependency relations that change move from being within-word to between-word, and involve the development of sublexemes). For example, there is a shift from *-ish* as an affix (in e.g. OE *cildisc* 'child-like') to a debonded form which can serve as a separate conversational turn (Norde (2009) and references therein). Also addressed is the fact that word-formation change can involve the loss of links (e.g. *-ster* no longer has a link associated with the concept 'female'), as well as recategorizations of particular links (e.g. from association to approximation in one of the sense relations of *-ish*).

---

[12] Gisborne (2017a) has a different method of representing sublexemes. We have changed his representation to be consistent with the representation we use. INF here stands for infinitive.

5.4.2 Building Nodes and Links

The creation of new nodes is an important aspect of the theory of WG in terms of a general theory of synchronic processing (Hudson, 2007, 2010). Here we address the question how some of the properties of node-building in WG may be relevant in thinking about change.

The first issue concerns the creation, and the degree of permanence, of token nodes in the network. Hudson (2007, 2010) suggests that token nodes are continually being built and forgotten by language users as they produce and process language. In this framework, 'processing takes place in "long term working memory"' where 'token nodes, for transient items of experience, form a constantly changing fringe on the edge of the permanent network' (Hudson, 2007, p. 42). The consequence of this is that utterance tokens are "'part of the grammar"' (Hudson, 2007, p. 44) and that these tokens 'may stabilize and become permanent' (Hudson, 2007, p. 45). In this regard, WG tokens are very like Bybeean exemplars (see Bybee (2013)).

Central to these claims is the notion of the isA link. In order to be processed, every new token of experience must be connected with some node in the permanent network, so that the token can inherit features. Consider a sentence such as (6):

(6)   The cat saw hte mouse.

In this sentence, in order to process word 4 (i.e. *hte*), we need to build a token node ('word4') and link it (via an isA link) to a type. The type we link it to is THE, and thus 'word 4' inherits all the properties we have stored for THE, except for the spelling, where our (default) expectations are overridden. As readers, we may have misjudged the writer's intention – she might have intended to produce *the cat saw her mouse* – but given the token that we have, we apply a Best-Fit principle (see below) to match the token to the type whose form and meaning provide the closest match given the context which, in the absence of other co(n)textual information to the contrary, would be THE.

Hudson (2010, p. 204) suggests that very many token nodes disappear almost immediately after they have been produced. Some, however, persist, and this persistence is said to be directly connected to the degree of effort required to interpret the token. A novel token, he argues, may persist until a similar token is encountered. At that point, the second token (call it 'word253') inherits its properties from 'word4'. His position is consistent with exemplar theory (see Section 4.3.4) and its relation to the organization of constructions (see Bybee (2010, 2013)) which has also been foregrounded in other recent work in CxG (e.g. Goldberg (2019)). In some accounts in both the CxG and WG traditions, parts of the language network are unstable, transient, and emergent. The question is how much of the network is like this. A strong exemplar position would propose that the entire network is unstable, constantly updated by every experience with language. A weak exemplar position would propose that there is a stable core with a less permanent fringe (see further Section 5.2.2).

In a discussion of the shift from word token to lexeme using the example of CATEGORY, Hudson writes:

> Thus what started as w1, a mere token pronounced (say) /katəgri/, may end as the new lexeme CATEGORY, a general concept to which future tokens can build an isA link. But it's important to remember that in this process the node doesn't change – on the contrary, its changed status comes from the fact that it **hasn't** changed by disappearing. (Hudson, 2010, p. 204, emphasis original)

While we are sympathetic to the general WG framework, we feel that this position regarding the shift during acquisition from token to type is inconsistent. First, even if we restrict our discussion to an individual's representation (and therefore to innovation in an individual's network, rather than replication across individuals which we argued in Section 2.3.1 is central for change), it does not seem possible that a node does not change as it moves from the less stable position as a token on the periphery towards a more stable position as a type. For instance, as Hudson (2007, 2010) rightly argues, tokens are massively rich and detailed: they are associated with a particular SP/W, occurring in a particular context, with specific cotext, on a given date, in a given location, and so on. All of these are specific associative links connected to particular tokens. Types lack many of these properties. Thus part of the shift from token to type must involve the loss of particular kinds of associative links.

Hudson (2010, pp. 205–206) also addresses how generalizations (which he calls 'schemas') are made. Schemas bring together properties shared by types. Creating a more schematic node also involves the creation of an isA relation, but to some extent there is some circularity here: the schema is created from the shared properties, but the isA link allows subtypes to inherit those shared properties. There are two relevant issues here. The first is that speakers tend to make low-level generalizations, and do not necessarily abstract to the most general level possible (Hudson (2007, pp. 49–50); also Hilpert (2015)). The second is that there is a significant difference between the isA relation between types and tokens, and the isA relation between types. This has to do with when the induction happens. Hudson (2010, p. 206) suggests that schema formation happens off-line, and concerns generalizations across memories, while low-level type formation (based on tokens of experience) happens online, as the tokens are being processed. This is a rather different concept of 'schema' than the one in CxG, which has essentially the same organization as the more specific construction (i.e. it is a unit that involves a conventionalized pairing for form and meaning).

A final feature of WG that we need to introduce here is the notion of binding (Hudson, 2007, pp. 46–50). There are many properties of binding in WG. We select only those that are particularly relevant to understanding language change. The most important of these has already been mentioned: a given token of experience will be connected to a stored type. This binding of a token to a permanent type enables the token to be enriched because it will inherit (via isA) the properties of the type to which it is bound. An important question is how a language user knows to classify a particular token as 'belonging to' a particular type. Hudson (2007) suggests that language users make use of the Best-Fit Principle: they select the '**most active**' node (Hudson, 2007, p. 48, emphasis original). In WG nodes become active via spreading activation (see Section 4.3.4).

The point about the Best-Fit Principle is that it underscores the fact that, in every attempt to bind a token to a type, a range of options is available to the hearer. Specifically, in terms of the kinds of changes we are concerned with, a hearer will have a range of senses (linked to different types) which are active at the point of binding. Crucially, the link between a sense and a form intended by the speaker may not be the same link that is made by the hearer when the hearer tries to bind the token to a stored type. In terms of processing issues, Hudson (2007, p. 48) looks at the phenomenon of speech errors, but for the historical linguist, a more important feature is the possibility of a disjunction between the speaker's (intended) association of meaning to form and the hearer's (attempted) binding of form to meaning (cf. Section 2.3.1, especially the discussion around Table 2).

Generally with regard to building nodes and links, we observe that, in contrast to frameworks which propose a distinction between parts of language that are learned, and parts of language that are genetically endowed, both CxG and WG suggest that this categorical distinction should be replaced by a recognition of the continuum between linguistic items that are stored along with very rich contextual knowledge (usually tokens, in short-term memory) and those where the contextual knowledge associations are much less rich (usually types, in long-term memory; see Bybee (2010)).

5.4.3 Implications of WG for Network Theories of Change

Based on the ideas discussed in the subsections above, we suggest a number of more general observations about what change in the language network looks like. It is tempting to try to classify change as involving the creation, loss or recategorization of nodes and links (cf. Section 5.4.2 above and Trousdale (2025)). For example, evidence in corpus data of a neologism might suggest that a new node in the network has been created. In a WG-based view of language, this means that there is a new word-form associated with a new sense. New senses develop as language users experience new things in the world (e.g. inventions such as cellphones) which may be directly associated with new word-forms (e.g. neologisms such as *cellphone*). Similarly, a new node may be thought to be created when a word-form of uncertain etymology appears to be created from the phonological resources of the language. For instance, the word *cully* 'dupe, victim', in Dryden's epilogue to Lee's play *Mithridates, King of Pontus* (1678) is said to be associated with thieves' cant in the early Modern period, but the history of the word-form is unknown. However, developing a point made by Gisborne (2011) on the history of *will* in English, change in the language network can never really affect a node in isolation, simply because nodes themselves never occur in isolation. In order to be part of the network, the node must be linked in some way. Any new sense node is immediately linked to some other aspect of meaning ('cellphone' isA 'phone', for instance), and any new word-form will be connected to a sense (a 'sense of' relation from *cellphone* has the value 'cellphone').

A similar argument may be made in connection with the loss of nodes. For ease of exposition, we again consider lexical loss. An example is the loss of a word-form, for example, OE *forealdian*, 'to age, grow old'. This also entails the loss of the particular relation between form and meaning, since the sense persists, becoming associated with new word-forms. Relevant here too are the changes associated with lexicalization (Brinton and Traugott, 2005). Words such as *holiday* and *halibut* were originally composed of an adjective + noun sequence (*holy* + *day*, *holy* + *butte*, where *butte* is the name for a specific kind of flatfish). Over time, these sequences have lexicalized, and have significantly decreased internal compositionality and analyzability, certainly in the case of *halibut*. Those language users in earlier English who were the first to treat these word-forms as unanalyzed wholes had additional representations different from earlier generations of speakers, whose language networks involved links to *holy* and a dependency relation between the noun and its adjectival modifier. Similar changes have affected the representation of the meaning of these words in the network, since for many English speakers now there is no relation between 'holiday' and 'holy'. Thus these losses, which on the surface may appear to be changes to nodes alone, also involve changes in links.

We interpret the connection between node creation and the establishment of 'constructions' in WG terms as follows. Adopting the usage-based position that change is learning, and that learning is ongoing throughout the lifespan, understanding the process of learning provides a helpful first step for analyzing linguistic innovation in WG terms. The key issue is that humans are constantly having to categorize new tokens of experience. Each day we come across new things and we have to process them. Language is no different because we are constantly processing the products of other humans' linguistic creativity. The WG sequence for such learning is given below.[13] It elaborates the first two 'language user activities' associated with processes of innovation and change described in Table 2 in Section 2.3.1 above:

(i) A speaker produces an utterance including nodes that represent new tokens of linguistic experience. One such node is unfamiliar to the hearer.

(ii) The hearer perceives the tokens, including the unfamiliar one, and creates an isA link from that unfamiliar token node to the best-fit stored type.

(iii) Information flows from that type-node in the network down to the token. (The type node itself has other relational links to other nodes in the network, including an isA link to a further more general category.)

(iv) EITHER: The token node stays active on the fringes of the network for the hearer. Further experiences which require a similar classification on the part of the hearer can lead to the token node 'transforming' (which in historical linguistic terms, we might consider to be neoanalysis as a type node, a more permanent part of the individual's network).
OR: Should there be no such similar experiences, the token node does not persist. There is no further progression of the change, since no new type node has been created.

(v) The hearer speaks, and the potential for further learning experiences repeats from (i).

Where a new type node is created, (i.e. where the process develops to (iv), this is a case of idiolectal innovation. In some cases, this idiolectal innovation may involve the transmission of forms that have existed for some time among other speakers, but not in the case of the particular language user whose idiolect is being described. In other cases, it may represent a development which is not attested elsewhere in the speech community. Let us consider each step in turn. Recall that an important step in the innovation process is the creation of a new type node that is inheriting properties from a more general and established type node. For clarity we use $type_e$ for the existing/established type, and $type_n$ for

---

[13] This is the typical case. Martin Hilpert (personal communication) points out that in salient contexts, type creation may occur as the result of one encounter with a new token. Repetition is critical for type entrenchment.

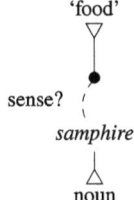

Figure 7 Conjecturing the meaning of the new word *samphire*

the new type that has just been created from generalization across the tokens of experience. What are the differences that exist between type$_e$ and type$_n$? Much will depend on the nature of the token and the contexts in which the innovation is occurring. For example, imagine a situation where language user A says the utterance in (7):

(7)   Have you ever eaten samphire?

to language user B, who has never heard the word *samphire* before. In order to process (7), user B will create a token node for the phonetic form of *samphire*, and link it to the type node 'noun'. They do this because they recognize *samphire* as the object of *eaten*, and objects are typically nouns. On the meaning side, 'samphire' will form an isA link to 'food'. This is modelled in Figure 7, where the dotted line represents a plausible connection between an experienced but unknown form and a potential meaning.

Should user B encounter more linguistic data involving *samphire*, this may become a permanent type in the network. This example illustrates the kind of innovation where a speaker learns a 'new' word which has existed for some time in the idiolects of other speakers of English, but not in the idiolect of user B.

What about cases which involve the creation of new grammatical expressions? We will see that the processes involved are very similar. In cases of grammatical change, the new token of experience may appear not to involve the learning of a new word. Instead, language users seem to imply or infer grammatical meanings of words that are, in other contexts, used lexically. This is clearly reminiscent of grammaticalization. But what the WG account does is think not so much about the trajectory of single items, but of the other factor in grammaticalization that Meillet (1958 [1912], p. 147) wrote about – that grammaticalization can involve 'la façon de grouper les mots', the way in which words can be brought together in set sequences. In WG (and also CxG), this process is about how the node fits in the network.

In WG terms, then, at the very beginning of grammatical change (i.e. at the point of innovation) a language user creates a token node whose form is best-matched to the form of an existing type-node, but whose meaning is less well-aligned to the type node's meaning. Specifically, the meaning of the token picks out one aspect of the meaning of the type node, part of the meaning which is not conventional and semantic, but contextual and pragmatic. We relate this to the notion of the sublexeme in WG.

Recall that the characterization of the sublexeme is one in which a particular node inherits some properties from a more general node, but also has properties that distinguish it from the more general node. We saw this in the WG analysis of idioms in Section 4.4. Recall also that from a WG perspective constructions are network fragments (Section 4.4). Word Grammar is concerned not with the grammar of words in isolation, but with words and their relations, and this is where there is an especially strong connection with CxG. More specifically, in the context of language change, new constructions can be seen as weakly entrenched network fragments. That is, in cases of language change, speakers in a linguistic community appear to be converging on a set of associations that a word (or in some cases, a set of words) has. Indeed, almost everything that is 'new' has its roots in associations with extant words, and many grammatical/procedural constructions in English initially develop through idiomaticization.

Here we develop the idea that change involves the creation of sublexemes, and that it involves not just change to nodes, but to nodes and links simultaneously. We illustrate with reference to the development of the *Way*-construction. We have chosen this example as it has been well-documented in the (Diachronic) CxG literature, and thus allows for comparisons between WG and CxG accounts (the latter being provided by, among others, Israel (1996) and Traugott and Trousdale (2013)). The early history of the *Way*-construction involves the sedimentation of a particular pattern. The development involved the bringing together of different argument structure patterns. In late ME, the relevant constructions involve a) intransitive motion with path (*he wente his wei*) and b) transitive acquisition (*Joseph anon nom his pas* 'Joseph immediately took his way'). These input strings were variable, involving lexemes such as *pas* and determiners other than possessives (*make an eesie way to vs* 'make an easy way to us'). Figures 8 and 9 provide representations for the intransitive motion and the transitive acquisition networks, respectively, in late ME. In these (and later) figures, a+ marks a pre-adjunct, +a marks a post-adjunct and c marks a complement. (Hudson, 2010).

By the end of the seventeenth century, the textual data suggest a new, more fixed, construction had developed, partially different from both the intransitive and transitive 'inputs': *way* now has to be the complement of a subtype of pronoun (e.g. *his*). There is a new restriction on the kind of dependency that is

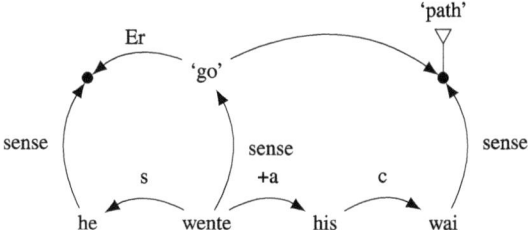

Figure 8 WG network for intransitive motion with a path in late ME

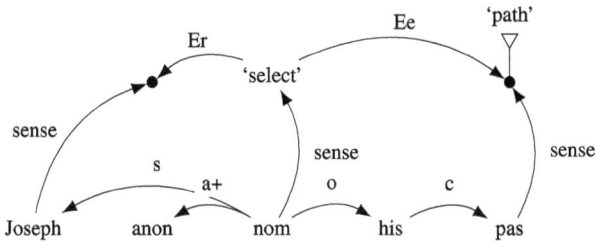

Figure 9 WG network for transitive acquisition of a path in late ME

allowed. Another development is that the verb must have a complement taken from a limited set of categories (typically a preposition, though other categor- ies such as adverbs (e.g. *there*) are possible). This is the 'oblique' argument in CxG terms. It is another kind of fixed structure in the network. An analysis of the development in WG terms would be as follows: the development of the '*way*-construction' involves the development of an idiom that has a sublexeme of WAY as a fixed part of the structure. We can call this sublexeme WAY$_{/POSS}$ because it must be the (post)dependent of a head that has the form of a posses- sive. But recall that idioms in WG don't simply involve a single sublexeme: they also involve a set of relations around the sublexeme:

 (i) The head of WAY$_{/POSS}$ must be the object dependent of the verb.
 (ii) That verb must have a further dependent that is typically a preposition.
(iii) Although WAY$_{/POSS}$ is the complement of the object, it is not the theme argument of the verb in the semantics (known in WG as the Ee relation), because the verb is monovalent – in other words, it just has an agent argu- ment (known in WG as the Er relation). Thus there is a mismatch – the default link between the o (object) relation in the syntax and the Ee relation in the semantics is overriden in this case.

These changes result in a network for the (early) ModE *way*-construction as given in Figure 10. Figure 10 is left deliberately schematic, to show the generalized pattern.

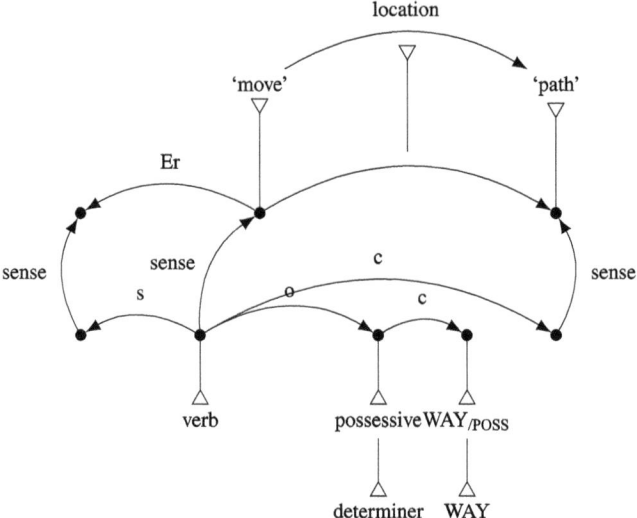

location

'move'   'path'

Er

sense   sense   c   sense

s   o   c

verb   possessive WAY/POSS

determiner   WAY

Figure 10 A WG analysis of the (Early) Modern English *way*-construction

The key issue here is that the 'construction' is a network centered around a sublexeme. The regular lexeme WAY does not have the precise network configuration that WAY/POSS has. By activating the WAY/POSS node, language users activate the network of links around the node and align a formal configuration with a set of meanings.

5.5 Summary

We have addressed three issues that are background for our main data discussion in Section 6. Building on some principles of change discussed in Section 2.3 relevant to our discussion of networks, Section 5.2 focused on data and methodology, especially qualitative and qualitative approaches to change. In Section 5.3 we considered constructional approaches to language change and recharacterized constructionalization, and in Section 5.4 we looked at approaches to change in WG. Having outlined the various issues in this way, we are now in a position to consider our case study on English causal connectives.

6 A Case Study: The Rise of Causal Connectives in English

6.1 Why This Case Study

In this section, we present a qualitative account of the rise in English of causal connectives from the ninth century to the present. Connectives are markers of textual relationships, and therefore illustrate networks well at both micro and macro levels. They can be used to highlight distinctions in the approaches of DCxG and WG. We focus on *because*, the currently most frequently used causal connective. A DCxG approach is presented below in Section 6.2, and a diachronic WG approach in Section 6.3. Section 6.4 summmarizes.

6.2 English Causal Connective Constructions and Their History

The contemporary causal connectives network is outlined in Section 6.2.1. Developments from OE on are presented from a constructional perspective in Section 6.2.2, and in Section 6.2.3, some reflections on DCxG and language change are presented.

6.2.1 Contemporary English Causal Connectives as a Dynamic Constructional Network

Connectives are markers that speakers use to signal the link intended between discourse segment 1 and discourse segment 2. Fraser (2006) (and elsewhere) calls them Discourse Markers, but that term is also more broadly used for pragmatic markers like *y'know* (see Schiffrin (1987)), so the more explicit term Discourse Structuring Markers (Traugott, 2022) is preferable for connectives. On our analysis, Discourse Structuring Markers are constructions with connective syntax and pragmatic discourse functions such as reasoning, elaboration, and contrast.

We consider linguistic 'causation' to be 'a relation that is interpreted *by the speaker* as being a relation between cause and effect' (Degand, 1994, p. 108, ft. 1, italics original). In other words, it is an inferential relation that is distinct from referential 'causality' in the physical world. Our focus is on causal connectives. This for the most part excludes consideration of links with adjuncts of result such as *therefore, so* (see Lenker (2007)), reason such as *for this reason, consequently* (see Mittwoch, Huddleston, Collins, and Pullum (2002, p. 726)) and periphrastic causatives such as *force X to* (see Kemmer and Verhagen (2005)). We also exclude prosodic factors in spoken discourse as speech is unavailable in most historical texts.

In standard contemporary written English, the causal connectives include *because, since, for*, and *as. Because* is the most frequent in speech (Lenker (2007, p. 195), citing Altenberg (1984, p. 45)). As discussed below, the set of causal connectives was significantly different in earlier English.

In a well-known study of multiple interpretations of modals like *must* and connectives like *because* and *if,* Sweetser (1990, p. 78) proposed that they could be understood in three conceptual domains that depend on a pragmatically motivated choice between viewing the conjoined clauses as representing real-world 'content' units, epistemic assessments pointing to the speaker's degree of certainty, or speech acts pointing to the speaker's reason for saying something. Sweetser (1990, p. 78) gives the constructed examples in (8) with *since*, a connective that has the added property of evoking given information.

(8)   (a) *Since* John wasn't there, we decided to leave a note for him.
       (b) *Since* John isn't here, he has (evidently) gone home.
       (c) *Since* we're on the subject, when was George Washington born?

According to Sweetser, (8a) expresses socio-physical real-world reasoning and is 'contentful', (8b) expresses the speaker's logical conclusion ('epistemic'), and (8c) expresses the fact that being on the subject enables the speaker to ask the question ('speech act').

Beyond such pragmatic factors, recurrent topics in the literature on causal connectives concern subordinate-coordinate use. Although causal clauses are traditionally thought to be syntactically subordinate, a clear-cut distinction between subordinate and coordinate use may be overridden by functional pragmatic factors, especially in conversation. Compare (9) with (10). Subordinate (9; from Schiffrin (1987, p. 211, bolding added)) gives the reason why the terrace is wet.

(9)   The terrace is wet **because** it rained.

Non-subordinate (10; from Schiffrin (1987, p. 212, bolding original)) gives an explanation of why SP finds it hard to remain friends with both sides. (Note that reduced conversational *cause* is used.)

(10)   It's very hard t'remain friends with both sides. **Cause** you're afraid t'say something, or this or that.

Diessel and Hetterle (2011, p. 2) find that, cross-linguistically, causal clauses are often analyzable as co-ordinate clauses. They are less likely than temporal and conditional adverbial clauses to be subordinate in conversation, where they tend to be 'only loosely associated with the main clause'.

Less frequently discussed is that *because*-clauses may be used independently as stand-alone clauses as in (11; Schiffrin (1987, p. 200, italics and bolding original)):

(11)   Irene: *That*'s asinine, Henry
       Henry: **Because** you don't understand.

Such independent clauses with subordinate form can in context be considered to be instantiations of simple, mono-clausal assertions, rather than to be lacking complex structure. Two other recurrent topics in the literature on causal connectives will be only marginally touched on below. One is clause order. In contemporary English, causal clauses, especially *because*-clauses, tend to follow the main clause (Diessel and Hetterle (2011); Ford (1993); Quirk et al. (1985, p. 1106)). Ford (1993, p. 142) attributes this to the fact that, in conversation, causal clauses are used to 'present background or motivation in interactional moves' rather than having a 'discourse orientational function'.

The other topic concerns hypothesized macro links with conditional (*if-then*), concessive (*although*), and contrast (*but*) expressions (see Sweetser (1990) on causal, adversative and conditional conjunctions, and Cause, Condition, Concession, Contrast, the title of Couper-Kuhlen and Kortmann (2000)). That there are macro-links is supported by evidence such as the following. On the form side, adverbial clauses allow syntactic subordination. In some languages, they may be encoded the same way (Kortmann (1997)). On the meaning side, they express relations of circumstance. Causal expressions may pragmatically presuppose conditionals. For example, *the streets are wet, because it rained* presupposes 'if it rains, the streets will be wet' (König and Siemund 2000, p. 343, 351). Concessives have been interpreted as 'inoperant cause' (Couper-Kuhlen and Kortmann (2000, p. 2)). Adverbial clauses take the speaker's (or subject of consciousness's) stance into account, so all involve subjectivity Traugott (2010); they also all involve multiple points of view and are polyphonic (Couper-Kuhlen and Kortmann (2000, p. 4)) and therefore involve intersubjectivity (see Brems, Ghesquière, and Van de Velde (2014)).

From a constructional perspective, contemporary English causal connectives can be considered to be part of a macro-network of abstract adverbial constructions that include complex clause configurations with causal, conditional and other adverbial functions. In contemporary English a CauseEffect subschema can be posited with two constructions, one 'causal', the other 'result'. The chief micro-constructions associated with the Causal Construction are *because*, *since*, *for*, those with the Result Construction are *so*, *therefore*. Schiffrin (1987, p. 204) illustrates the cause-result distinction with (12); emphasis of *cause* and *so* original:

(12)   We were going up t'see uh . . . my- our son tonight, but we're not **cause** the younger one's gonna come for dinner . . . **So** that's out.

Assuming an adverbial macro-schema that encompasses a set of linked adverbial subschemas, a partial constructional representation of the partonymic set-member relationships among members of this macro-schema can be represented as in Figure 11. The representation is partial, as there are additional

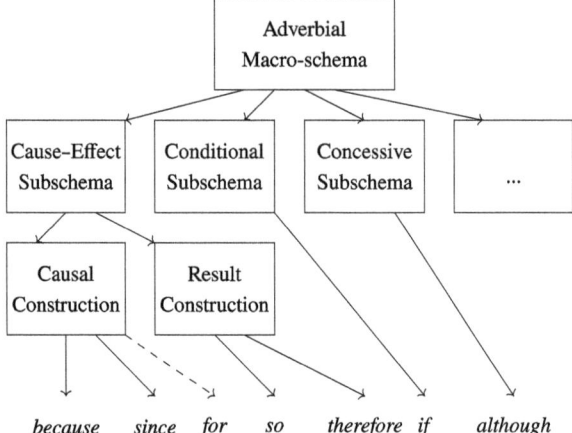

Figure 11 A partial constructional representation of set-member relationships among members of the Adverbial macro-schema in contemporary English

subschemas such as contrast, and additional connectives such as *as* (causal) and *thus* (result). The broken line to *for* indicates that it is obsolescing.

In speech or writing, the subschemas in Figure 11 are assembled (cf. Section 3.2) with complex clause configurations, which are of two main types, subordinate and coordinate. These complex clause types are on a continuum.

6.2.2 A DCxG Perspective on Major Changes in the History of the Causal Connective Network

Causal connectives in OE were very different in form and to some extent in function from those in contemporary English. Typically, they had a form of the type *for TH-*. These are frozen, non-compositional connectives originating in a Proto-Germanic demonstrative pronoun *se* in the dative (*þæm*) or instrumental (*þy, þon*) case. According to the *Dictionary of Old English Corpus* (DOEC), typical causal connective forms are *for þæm* (e.g. (13a)), sometimes with the subordinator (glossed as SUBR) *þe* (e.g. (13b)), *for þy* (e.g. (14)), *for þon*, and in later OE *for þæt*. In (13a), the first instance of *þæm* functions as an inflected demonstrative in a prepositional phrase, while the second functions as part of a fixed connective expression.

(13)   (a)   swiþost he for   ðider ... for þæm horshwælum for ðæm hie
               chiefly he went there ... for the   walruses   for that they
               habbað swiþe æþele ban   on hiora toþum
               have   very   fine   ivory in their tusks
               'Chiefly he went there ... for the walruses, because they have
               very fine ivory in their tusks' (c880, Orosius 1.1.14.30; DOEC)

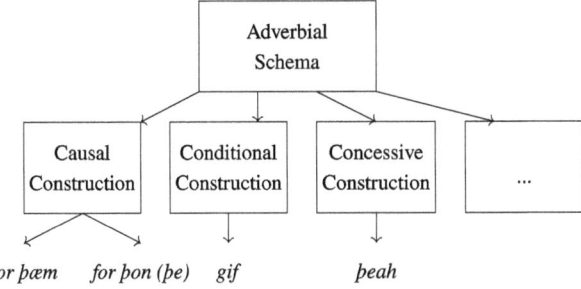

Figure 12 A partial constructional representation of set-member relationships among members of the Adverbial schema in OE

(b) Æfter þæm Romane wunnon on   Cartaine,   for þæm
    after that Romans fought   against Carthaginians, for that
    þe   hie frið   abrocen hæfdon
    SUBR they peace broken had
    'After that, the Romans fought against the Carthaginians, because
    they had broken the peace' (c880, Orosius 7.97.15; DOEC)

Note that in both examples the causal clause follows the main clause.

All three forms *for þæm, forþon, forþy* (+subordinator) could be potentially ambiguous with result meanings. In other words, the cause-result distinction was not formally made. However, most examples are readily disambiguated in context (Lenker, 2007, pp. 202–205), as in (14), which concerns funerary customs among the Estonians:

(14)   hyt motan habban eall; &   for ðy þær beoð þa swiftan hors
       it might have   all; and for that there be   the swift   horses
       ungefoge dyre
       extremely valuable
       'they may keep it (the dead man's property) all, and therefore swift
       horses are extremely valuable there' (c880, Orosius 1.1.12; DOEC)

A partial representation of set-member relations among types of adverbial constructions in OE is provided in Figure 12.

Note, in comparison to Figure 11 (representing contemporary English), there is no Cause-Effect Subschema, since the contemporary patterns which distinguish cause and result were not available to OE speakers using this *for TH*-system to signal causal connectivity. Therefore, in describing the OE partial network, we refer to the generalization above the level of Causal Construction simply as an Adverbial Schema. (Recall from Section 3.2 that the labels for schematic levels are our linguistic analyses of groups of generalizations in the data.) In later ME and EModE the *for TH-* connectives were replaced by connectives that had different forms and that distinguished cause and effect. The system represented in Figure 11 emerged.

A far less frequently used causal marker in OE is *siþþan* 'since', derived from temporal 'from the time that'. Like contemporary causal *since*, it is mainly used with temporal meaning. When used as a causal, it signals that the upcoming clause alludes to given information, and it typically precedes the main clause. In (15) *siþþan* is used to translate a Latin ablative absolute 'given that' construction and follows *þa* 'then', which translates *postquam* 'after that', but the inference is strong that a causal relation is intended.

(15)   þa,   siþþan he irre   wæs &   gewundod, he ofslog micel þæs folces
        then since   he angry was and wounded, he slew   many of-the host
        'Then, since he was angry and wounded, he slew many of the host'
        (c880 Orosius 1.84.19; DOEC)

Clauses introduced by *siþþan* 'since' are not always clearly subordinate in OE (Kemenade, 1994, p. 137).

By the late fourteenth century, in southern ME, the *for TH-* causals had largely been replaced by *because*, bare *for* and *since*. Use of *therefore* to mark result had also emerged. Causal *for* appears in OE, but not bare without a following *TH-* form. Although the frozen *for TH-* connectives were not compositional, by hypothesis they were analyzable as *for* followed by a form like the demonstratives *þæm, þy, þon*. The form *since* originates in the ME version of OE *siþþan*, specifically ME *sithen* 'after' + *-es*, an adverb-forming suffix. The shift away from the OE system was slower in northern English. For example, in the York Plays of the later fifteenth century (Beadle, 2009), the dominant causal conjunctions are *for* and *sen* 'since' in various spellings, although an occasional *bycause* is attested. Lenker (2007, pp. 216–217, 222) regards the ME and EModE periods as periods of experimentation with various causal connectives, including *for as much as*, which has not survived. She says (p. 222) that *because* came to be used as the default causal connector only after 1750, when it supplanted *for*.

Use of *because* as a connective from the fourteenth century on suggests that neoanalysis and constructionalization of *by cause (that)* had occurred. It is particularly interesting in part because the noun *cause* is a borrowing. The languages of education and administration during the ME period were, to varying degrees, Latin and Continental French (Burnley (1992); Townend (2006)), so literate authors were well versed in those languages. At the time, the most frequently used causal conjunction in Continental French was subordinating *parceque*. Like OE *for TH-* constructions, it originated in a pronominal expression (literally 'by this that') but came to be a fixed expression. Given its similarity to the OE construction, it is unlikely that Continental French was the source of the English shifts away from causal connectives with *TH-*. A possible source was Insular French (also known as 'Anglo-Norman' and 'Anglo-French'; see Wogan-Browne (2009)). Using the term 'Anglo-Norman', Ingham (2012) argues that during the ME period Anglo-Norman did not undergo the standardization that Continental French did and developed different characteristics. One was the use of causal connectives with *cause*: initially, at the beginning of the fourteenth century *par cause que* 'by cause that', as in (16):

(16)   vous ne poez si toust venir per devers nous ... par cause que
        you not can so soon come by toward us   ... by cause that
        vostre mere   ... a   tresgrant meseise   de cuer
        your   mother ... has very.great complaint of heart
        'You cannot come to us so soon because your mother has a very serious
        heart complaint' (1326 Foedera 2, 623 [Ingham (2012, p. 113)])

It seems plausible to hypothesize that this Anglo-Norman connective was translated word for word ('calqued') in later ME as prepositional *by cause (that)*. However, the paucity of examples like (16) in Insular French texts suggests that connective *because* may actually have been an independent development in English and only marginally due to contact. We return to this in Section 6.3, on WG and the development of *because* in English.

The partial division of labor that emerged in the EModE period between *because* (content causal, often new information), *since* (known information) and *for* (explanation) appears to match aspects of multifunctionality in Latin and the Old (and now Modern) French systems. For example, Kroon (1995, pp. 131–132) posits some rough equivalences between Latin *quia/quod* and Sweetser's (1990) sociophysical cause, and *quoniam* with epistemic cause.

It has been suggested that during the EModE and LModE periods, various kinds of 'loosening' of ME subordinate structure are attested in texts. In EModE, instances appear in represented interaction of responses in which a causal clause is used independently, without a main clause. For example, both of Latronello's asides in (17) are independent clausal clauses, the first with *for*, the second with *because*:

(17)   Furtivo: No, 'tis well known, sir, I have a master the very picture of
        wisdom—
        Latronello: [Aside] For indeed he speaks not one wise word.

Furtivo: and no man but will admire to hear of his virtues—
Latronello: [Aside] *Because* he ne'er had any in all his life.
(1603-4 Middleton, *The Phoenix* III,i [Higashiizumi (2006, p. 91)])

Drawing on an earlier version of Evans (2007), Higashiizumi (2006) identifies the appearance of such uses as the development of 'insubordinate' uses, and suggests it is a case of degrammaticalization because a tighter subordinate structure becomes looser. This presupposes that *because* was primarily used as a subordinator. However, that is questionable because, as suggested in Section 6.2.1, the distinction between subordinate and insubordinate causals has never been sharp. It is more likely that independent uses are characteristic of interaction (see Diessel and Hetterle (2011)). They appear in question-and-answer routines already around 1000 in *Ælfric's Colloquy* (Garmonsway, 1991), and later in drama. It is likely that their appearance in the seventeenth century that Higashiizumi (2006) analyzes is correlated not with a change in the linguistic knowledge of speakers but in the conventions of relatively new genres such as drama, where asides are common. In fact, the polyphonic nature of adverbial circumstance constructions favors use by different speakers across turns.

A later development in LModE is use of *because* as a preposition with a bare adjective or noun. Both adjective and noun are used without modifiers and are said to be largely restricted to causal content pragmatics (Bergs (2017, p. 50), confirming Kanetani (2016)). Both are also used more subjectively than their full clausal counterparts (Bergs, 2017, p. 55). Bergs points out that in 2014 the American Dialect Society chose *because* as their word of the year for 2013 on the grounds that there had been an explosion of 'grammatical possibilities' in that year for *because*. He shows that in fact *because* + Adjective use appears (if only infrequently) already in the nineteenth century (see (18)) and increases moderately in frequency in the twentieth:

(18)   Bostonian appeals to history, and shows that Boston is first, *because oldest*. (1823 Neal, Randolph, a novel [Bergs (2017, p. 45)])

While *because* + Adjective is the oldest attested phrasal use of *because*, *because* + N is attested by 1940, for example, (19). It may have been influenced by *because of* + NP phrases.

(19)   this is a no-track mind. No-track *because infinity-track*. It's the mind of an idiot of genius. (1940 Huxley, Harper's Magazine [Bergs (2017, p. 45)])

Bergs sees *because* + Adjective/Noun as a largely twenty-first century phenomenon often associated with internet use, as in *because science*. There are also instances of *because* with a particle: *because duh, because wow*, and in tweets, with an idiomatic expression such as *you only live once* in acronymic form (*yolo*) (Bergs, 2017, p. 49). These do not have sense in the same way as *oldest* in (18) and *infinity-track* in (19) do. Instead they involve an expressive elaboration. The American Dialect Society's choice of *because* as the word of the year may be a case of 'innovation' understood as 'what I just noticed' (see Zwicky (2005) on the 'Recency Illusion' that what has just been noticed is a recent development). Bergs suggests that what was originally a *because* + Adjective collocation was gradually generalized to include nouns and particles leading to a schematic *because* X construction. Typically it is used in a complex clause construction, and presents 'a post-hoc justification and clarification' for the first clause (Bergs, 2017, p. 50).

The history of *because* illustrates several points that also pertain to the development of other adverbial connectors, such as *if* and *though*:

(i) In the languages of Western Europe, there has been a historical tendency toward monofunctionality (Kortmann (1997, p. 477)). Morphosyntactically, there is a tendency for one form to be chosen as the main marker (e.g. *because*). Semantically, there is a tendency toward loss of polyfunctionality of individual connectives (OE *for TH-* constructions, which expressed both cause and effect, were replaced by EModE by morphologically distinct *because* (cause) and *therefore* (effect)). See also Rissanen (2011) on the history of adverbial connections in English.

(ii) In the history of English, several connectives have been borrowed (Rissanen (2011)). Even if, as appears to be the case, *because* was not borrowed as a connective, it contains the borrowed noun *cause*.

(iii) All involve subjectification because an originally referential contentful expression is used to subjectively connect clauses. They also involve intersubjectification because they are polyphonic and activate multiple points of view in Addressees (see Chapter 4 in Traugott (2022)).

6.2.3 Some Reflections on DCxG and Language Change

Much work has been done in DCxG on ways in which CxG can contribute to historical linguistics. Here, we mention a few key points useful for a comparison between insights from DCxG and those of WG (Section 6.3.2). See further Section 7.

(i) The DCxG framework suggests that speakers learn form-meaning pairings (constructions) and the nodes and links between them. CxG foregrounds the analysis of changes in schemas and the growth and loss of (sometimes partonymic) subschemas.

(ii) DCxG provides a principled analysis of early and late stages in the development of constructions of any size or function, whether lexical argument structures like the English Ditransitive, or grammatical items like *must*.

(iii) A new 'construction' emerges when a social network of speakers shares and conventionalizes a new Cxn (e.g. use of *because* as a causal connective). The development of grammatical constructions correlates with early stages of 'clines of grammaticalization' such as are discussed in Hopper and Traugott (2003, p. 7). Some later changes, such as changes in distribution, frequency, or morphosyntactic form, typically correlate with constructional shifts.

So far in this section, we have assumed that a construct-i-con is a viable concept and have proposed how constructions that are 'in it' might be represented. We have also sketched the historical context of the development of causal connectives in English. In the next section, we explore the alternative approach to networks proposed in WG (Hudson, (2007, 2010)).

6.3 WG and the Development of *Because* in English

In this section we consider how the development of *because*, from the ME period on, as outlined in the preceding section, can be represented in WG terms. The analysis is presented in Section 6.3.1 and some reflections on WG and language change follow in Section 6.3.2. We use this section to provide an outline of how a grammatical change may be modelled using the network structures of WG. Specifically, we attempt to show how particular changes involve small adjustments to the earlier categorization of nodes and relations and/or the creation of new nodes and relations.

6.3.1 A WG Sketch of the Post-ME History of Because

It was observed in Section 6.2.2 above that the shift to *because* as a causative connective began in the ME period. In this section we provide a WG account of how such an innovation might be modelled in a network structure. We also examine the later changes involving *because*, where *because* appears to take non-nominal and non-verbal complements, as in *because hungry*.

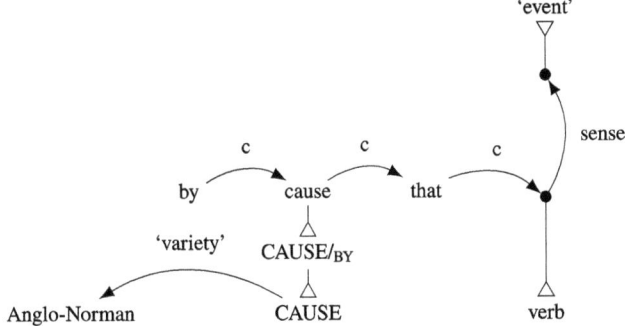

Figure 13 The WG CAUSE/$_{BY}$ sublexeme and its network

We begin with a reminder of the multilingual context in which some speakers of ME were operating. While the development of *because* may have been an 'English internal' one, it happened in a context in which various analogical models in at least two languages were available. First, as established in Section 6.2, there was the 'native' OE *for TH-* sequence, to which was added, in the ME period, patterns with bare *for*, and *since*. Second, there was the pattern influenced by Anglo-Norman *par cause que*. We noted in Section 6.2.2 that there appear to be few instances of this expression in the extant Anglo-Norman texts, so it is unlikely that the ME development is a direct calque. However, while the Anglo-Norman pattern may be too infrequent to serve as an analogical model, at the point in ME at which groups of language users were exposed to a range of variants (e.g. *for* X and *by cause (that)* X), especially in code-switching contexts, additional choice emerges in the meaning space, and the selection of one variant over another, as is known from sociolinguistic research, correlates with various speaker, addressee, context, and genre features.

As argued by Holmes and Hudson (2006) and Gisborne (2017a) in their treatment of idioms and of grammatical change, we propose that the early history of *because* (i.e. *by cause that*) involves the creation of a sublexeme. In other words, we suggest that essentially the same framework can be used for changes for the development of *because* as a causal connective, for the development of the *Way*-construction discussed in Section 5.4.3, and for the Romance future: in the early development of grammatical structures from lexical items, the creation of a sublexeme is an important step.

We hypothesize that the first stage in the process was that speakers associated a borrowed word *cause* with the category 'noun'. Then, a sublexeme of this new noun develops in a particular syntactic frame: *by cause that* X. As was the case with the *Way*-construction, a network is built around this sublexeme of CAUSE, as in Figure 13.

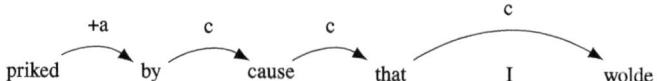

Figure 14 Partial WG syntactic analysis of *by cause that* in ME

We treat this as a sublexeme because it has certain properties that the (noun) lexeme does not have, namely that it can only be the complement of *by*, not of a pronoun like *the* or *his*, and that it must take *that* as its own complement.[14]

As with the early *Way*-construction, the set of nodes and links associated with *by cause that* is a weakly entrenched construction, which centres around a particular sublexeme. As more speakers make use of this linguistic structure, further changes develop in the late ME/EModE periods. One is that, like other prepositions in ME, *because* can take either the complementizer *that* (as in (20)) or a verb (as in (21)) as its complement. A second is that *by* and *cause* univerbate, retaining the earlier distributional properties of the head *by* (the univerbated *because* is a preposition, as in (22)). We illustrate both the earlier and later stages of this change with examples and figures that show a network for the forms undergoing change. Data are drawn from CMEPV, the *Corpus of Middle English Prose and Verse*. In each case, the example is followed by its analysis using the WG framework. Thus, Figure 14 is a partial representation of the syntactic network around *cause* in example 20.

(20)   ffaste haue I priked/ quod he for youre sake/ By cause/ that I
        'Fast have I ridden,' said he, 'for your sake, by cause that I
        wolde yow atake/
        wanted you overtake'
        'I rode quickly,' he said, 'for your sake, because I wanted to overtake
        you'
        (1396–1400 Chaucer, *Canon's Yeoman's Prologue*, Canterbury Tales.
        [CMEPV])

(21)   By cause he was of carpenteris craft, A litle ire   is in his hert ylaft
        By cause he was of carpenter's craft, a little anger is in his heart left
        'Because he was of the carpenter's craft, there was a little anger left
        in his heart' (1388–1392 Chaucer, *Reeve's Prologue*, Canterbury Tales
        [CMEPV])

---

[14] In WG, determiners are analyzed as a subtype of pronoun. See Hudson (1990) for further discussion.

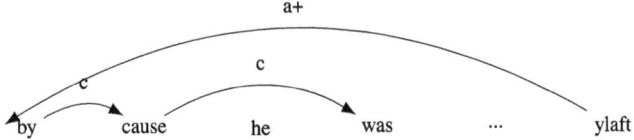

Figure 15 Partial WG syntactic analysis of *by cause* in ME

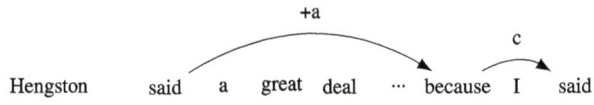

Figure 16 Partial WG syntactic analysis of *because* in ME

(22)   Hengston seide moche and strongely because y seide they hadde
       Hengston said   much and strongly because I said they had
       suche charters
       such charters
       'Hengston said a great deal and with great force because I said they
       had such charters'
       (c.1450 Letters and papers of John Shillingford, mayor of Exeter
       1447–1450. [CMEPV])

As can be seen from Figures 14–16, the changes involve a loss of a complement relation: the syntactic structures are simplified, in parallel with the loss of internal complexity in the univerbation to *because*.

A further step is the use in the early nineteenth century of *because* taking a complement that is not verbal or nominal. As example (18) in Section 6.2.2 above, we provided the following from 1823, cited by Bergs (2017, p. 45):

(23)   Boston is first, *because oldest.*

In this case, *because* is followed by an adjective. Such cases have been analysed as involving ellipsis (i.e. *Boston is first, because [Boston is] oldest*). In WG, ellipsis has been treated as involving unrealized words, which often isA words elsewhere in the utterance (Hudson, 2007, pp. 172–182). The claim is that in (23) there are in fact seven words, two of which (the second occurrence each of *Boston* and *is*) are phonologically unrealized but present in the syntactic structure. Because each is connected via an isA link to realized words, they inherit all the (grammatical) properties of those words, except where those defaults are overridden. Thus word2 (realized *is*) has the predicative complement *first* while word6 (unrealized *is*) has the predicative complement *oldest*.

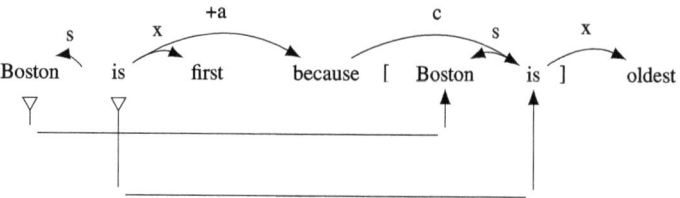

Figure 17 A WG network of *because* and ellipsis

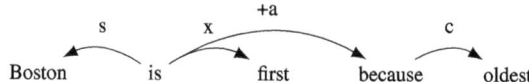

Figure 18 An alternative analysis of *because oldest*

This is illustrated in Figure 17, where 'x' is an abbreviation for 'xcomp' (predicative complement; see Section 5.4.1 above).

While there are advantages and drawbacks to this ellipsis analysis, the critical issue for analyzing language change is how this relates to processes of innovation. Certainly, the ellipsis analysis is not the only one that is available to the language user. Indeed, a hearer who encounters (23) could adopt a simpler analysis, namely that *because* is atypical among prepositions for allowing a greater range of word classes as dependents. In other words, while a speaker of (23) may be using an 'ellipsis' strategy, a hearer of (23) may analyze this as involving a simpler dependency between a preposition and an adjective as in Figure 18.

This would also explain more recent patterns such as (24) where the elided structure involves a predicative that is headed by a preposition:

(24)   I'm so happy today because in love.

The development of *because* + N tokens (e.g. *because science)* is straight-forwardly handled in WG since *because* is a preposition, and prepositions frequently take nouns (or pronouns) as their dependents.

6.3.2 Some Reflections on WG and Language Change

In thinking about how WG connects with linguistic change as characterized in Section 2.3, we consider the following issues to be primary.

(i) The WG framework suggests that speakers learn classifications of both nodes and links, from phonology through to discourse (though we have focussed mainly on syntax and semantics). From the perspective of grammatical change, WG foregrounds the analysis of micro-changes in individual representations, and changes in word-to-word dependencies.

(ii) WG provides a principled treatment of early and late stages in the development of grammatical expressions. This allows the analyst to zoom in on how particular configurations change as new constructions (understood as network fragments) arise.

(iii) Specifically, a new 'construction' emerges when a social network of speakers shares the same fragment of a linguistic network built around a new sublexeme. If that sublexeme is linked to procedural meanings (as is the case with English CAUSE/$_{BY}$ described above, or Latin HABERE/$_{INF}$ (Gisborne, 2017a)), then we see this as the early stage of the development of a grammatical construction. In more traditional terms, this may appear to be the development of a grammatical word (= the sublexeme) from a lexical word, and so a case of early grammaticalization (Hopper and Traugott, 2003). However, our focus has been not just on the sublexeme, but on the network of connections around the sublexeme (i.e. on links as much as on nodes), following Gisborne (2011).

6.4 Summary

We have illustrated some properties of the English causal connective network and changes to it from OE to the present day. We suggested how the changes can be conceptualized in terms of DCxG and WG. In the process, we proposed ways in which WG has and is being developed to account for language change.

7 Concluding Remarks

We have compared two cognitive approaches to networks, with focus on how they model changes in networks. Both are usage models. Both contribute to teasing apart the role of the individual and the group by distinguishing between speaker or hearer-based innovations and communal changes. Both can address the networks and changes to them equally well. However, their architecture suggests different foci, most especially when conceptualized in diachronic terms.

From a constructionalist perspective such as is articulated in Goldberg (2003) and Diessel (2019), linguistic knowledge is shared knowledge stored in a construct-i-con. The construct-i-con is a set of networked form-meaning pairings (constructions) that are conventionalized (a social phenomenon). Each construction is a complex node, externally connected to other constructions via associative links and hierarchical relations. Links exist within constructions too (e.g. the symbolic link between form and meaning).

The architecture of CxG posits that knowledge of language is knowledge of constructions: conventionalized form-meaning pairings. In its diachronic dimension, the focus is on development of conventionalized structures, some of which can be quite abstract and schematic. Focus on conventionalized structure motivates the hypotheses that there is a distinction between innovation and change (see Section 2.3.1) and that constructionalizations occur as well as constructional shifts (Section 5.3.1). Much work in DCxG is concerned with understanding quantitative approaches to constructional change, with a particular interest in foregrounding the importance of frequency in both the entrenchment and conventionalization of changes.

By contrast, the architecture of WG posits that knowledge of language is knowledge of words and their relations. In the diachronic dimension of WG the focus is primarily on innovation in the creation of new nodes and links; the loss of new nodes and links; shifts in entrenchment of nodes and links; and reclassification of nodes and links (see Section 4.4). Unlike in DCxG, issues regarding frequency, community and conventionalization have not as yet been of central concern in diachronic applications of WG, though there is work on the social dimension of WG (Hudson, 1996), as well as attempts to link frequency changes to variation and change in the structure of the language network (Hudson, 1997a).

From a WG perspective such as is articulated in Hudson (2007), language is a network only of nodes (words) and links within and between words. There are no complex nodes. Unlike in CxG, networks in WG are organized around dependencies and not constituency structures. A construction is 'a particular configuration of words related by dependencies defined in terms of more or less specific types of word and dependency' (Hudson, 2007, p. 156). In such a framework, change is change to nodes and links. While WG recognizes that 'language is a social fact' (Hudson, 2007, p. 1), its focus on the understanding of conceptual structure means its primary goal is to understand individual knowledge.

We believe that the more precise we can be about the nature of the nodes and links in a given usage-based theory of language, the better we will be able to understand the specific dynamics regarding the mechanisms of innovation. Word Grammar has a well-developed theory of the nature of nodes and links. It requires the additional feature of the sublexeme to account for patterns which are otherwise considered as idiomatic chunks (a type of construction) in CxG. We have drawn attention to claims that some of the consequences of a constituent-based structure in CxG may be problematic given what we know about the organization of conceptual networks.

In keeping with the spirit of the *Elements* series, our presentation has been exploratory. Among the many open questions that remain are:

(i) How can changes across networks that are conceptually related best be accounted for? For example, cause has often been linked semantically to abstract domains such as condition, concession, and contrast (e.g. Couper-Kuhlen and Kortmann (2000)). As we have shown, cause and result, which might appear to be moderately separate domains, were initially both expressed by the same morphology in English, but were later distinguished by for example, *because* and *therefore*.

(ii) How best can quantitative shifts be accounted for from the perspectives of both DCxG (see Hilpert (2021)) and approaches to network change in WG (see Hudson (1997a, 1997b))?

(iii) How best can knowledge of social factors such as contact or genre, and of inferences come to be associated over time with particular assemblies of constructions or words be accounted for? For an overview of synchronic explorations of the relationships of constructions with register and genre, see Nikiforidou and Fischer (2015).

(iv) What does psycholinguistic work tell us about diachrony that supports one model or the other? We note that as CxG has moved from a more 'traditional' linguistic practice to a more psycholinguistic one, the characterization of a 'construction' has naturally and rightly evolved over time (compare e.g. Goldberg (1995, 2006, 2019)). These different characterizations have an effect on understanding what is meant by change. There is considerable interest in investigating psycholinguistic processes in language change (see Grossman and Noveck (2015) and Hundt, Mollin, and Pfenninger (2017)).

Contributions in the *Elements* series are intended to be short and provocative, suggesting new potential directions for research. In this contribution, we have not been able to cover all the interesting new developments in DCxG, especially with regard to the detailed quantitative analysis that is being undertaken. Nor have we explored work in other related subfields of cognitive linguistics (like the conventionalization-and-entrenchment model of Schmid (2020)). We see such research as adding significantly to our understanding of the usage-based model of language change, and a longer monograph on networks and language change would address these topics (and more general work in network science) in detail. Our goal has been modest: to look at what is understood by change in network representation in two closely related subdisciplines of cognitive linguistics, namely CxG and WG, and the extent to which close, qualitative analysis of textual material can be adduced to theorize about language change in a usage-based framework. We hope we have furthered the debate on how best to account for changes within networks.

References

Altenberg, B. (1984). Causal linking in spoken and written English. *Studia Linguistica*, *38*, 20–69.

Andersen, H. (2001). Actualization and the (uni)directionality of change. In H. Andersen (Ed.), *Actualization: Linguistic Change in Progress* (pp. 225–248). Amsterdam: Benjamins.

Anderson, J. R. (1983). A spreading activation theory of memory. *Journal of Verbal Learning and Verbal Behavior*, *22*, 261–295.

Anthonissen, L. (2021). *Individuality in Language Change*. Berlin: De Gruyter Mouton.

Anthonissen, L., & Petré, P. (2020). Individuality in complex systems: A constructionist approach. *Cognitive Linguistics*, *31*, 185–212.

Anttila, R. (2003). Analogy: The warp and woof of cognition. In B. D. Joseph & R. D. Janda (Eds.), *The Handbook of Historical Linguistics* (pp. 425–440). Oxford: Blackwell.

Auer, P., & Pfänder, S. (2011). Constructions: *Emergent* or *emerging?* In P. Auer & S. Pfänder (Eds.), *Constructions: Emerging and Emergent* (pp. 1–21). Berlin: De Gruyter.

Barabási, A.- L. (2008). *Network Science*. Cambridge: Cambridge University Press.

Barðdal, J. (2008). *Productivity: Evidence from Case and Argument Structure in Icelandic*. Amsterdam: Benjamins.

Barðdal, J., Smirnova, E., Sommerer, L., & Gildea, S. (Eds.). (2015). *Diachronic Construction Grammar*. Amsterdam: Benjamins.

Baumann, A., & Sommerer, L. (2018). Linguistic diversification as a long-term affect of asymmetric priming: An adaptive dynamic approach. *Language Dynamics and Change*, *8*, 253–296.

Beadle, R. (2009). *The York Plays: A Critical Edition of the York Corpus Christi Play as Recorded in British Library Additional MS 35290* (No. 23). Oxford: Oxford University Press.

Beckner, C., Blythe, R., Bybee, J., Christiansen, M., Croft, W., Ellis, N., Holland, J., Ke, J., Larsen-Freeman, D., & Schoenemann, T. (2009). Language is a complex adaptive system: Position paper. In N. C. Ellis & D. Larsen-Freeman (Eds.), *Language as a Complex Adaptive System* (pp. 1–26). Oxford: Wiley-Blackwell.

Bergs, A. (2017). Because science! Notes on a variable conjunction. In E. Seoane, C. Acuña-Fariña, & I. Palacios-Martínez (Eds.), *Subordination in English: Synchronic and Diachronic Perspectives* (pp. 43–60). Berlin: De Gruyter Mouton.

Blake, N. (1992). Introduction. In N. Blake (Ed.), *The Cambridge History of the English Language Volume II, 1066–1476* (pp. 1–22). Cambridge: Cambridge University Press.

Blakemore, D. (1987). *Semantic Constraints on Relevance*. Oxford: Blackwell.

Börjars, K., Vincent, N., & Walkden, G. (2015). On constructing a theory of grammatical change. *Transactions of the Philological Society, 113*, 363–382.

Brems, L., Ghesquière, L., & Van de Velde, F. (Eds.). (2014). *Intersubjectivity and Intersubjectification in Grammar and Discourse* (2nd revised ed.). Amsterdam: Benjamins.

Brinton, L. J., & Traugott, E. C. (2005). *Lexicalization and Language Change*. Cambridge: Cambridge University Press.

Budts, S., & Petré, P. (2020). Putting connections center stage in Diachronic Construction Grammar. In L. Sommerer & E. Smirnova (Eds.), *Nodes and Networks in Diachronic Construction Grammar* (pp. 317–351). Amsterdam: Benjamins.

Burnley, D. (1992). Lexis and semantics. In N. Blake (Ed.), *The Cambridge History of the English Language Volume II, 1066–1476* (pp. 409–499). Cambridge: Cambridge University Press.

Bybee, J. L. (1994). The grammaticization of zero: Asymmetries in tense and aspect systems. In W. Pagliuca (Ed.), *Perspectives on Grammaticalization* (pp. 235–254). Amsterdam: Benjamins.

Bybee, J. L. (2010). *Language, Usage and Cognition*. Cambridge: Cambridge University Press.

Bybee, J. L. (2013). Usage-based theory and exemplar representations of constructions. In T. Hoffmann & G. Trousdale (Eds.), *The Oxford Handbook of Construction Grammar* (pp. 49–69). New York: Oxford University Press.

Chomsky, N. (1995). *The Minimalist Program*. Cambridge, MA: MIT Press.

Claridge, C. (2012). From manuscript to printing: Transformations of genres in the history of English. In T. Nevalainen & E. C. Traugott (Eds.), *The Oxford Handbook of the History of English* (pp. 304–313). New York: Oxford University Press.

Collins, A., & Loftus, E. (1975). A spreading-activation theory of semantic processing. *Psychological Review, 82*, 407–428.

Couper-Kuhlen, E., & Kortmann, B. (Eds.). (2000). *Cause, Condition, Concession, Contrast: Cognitive and Discourse Perspectives*. Berlin: Mouton de Gruyter.

Creider, C., & Hudson, R. (1999). Inflectional morphology in Word Grammar. *Lingua, 107*, 163–187.

Croft, W. (2001). *Radical Construction Grammar: Syntactic Theory in Typological Perspective*. Oxford: Oxford University Press.

Croft, W. (2005). Logical and typological arguments for Radical Construction Grammar. In J.-O. Östman & M. Fried (Eds.), *Construction Grammars: Cognitive Grounding and Theoretical Extensions* (pp. 273–314). Amsterdam: Benjamins.

Curzan, A. (2017). Periodization in the history of the English language. In A. Bergs & L. Brinton (Eds.), *The History of English: Historical Outlines from Sound to Text* (pp. 8–35). Berlin: De Gruyter Mouton.

Degand, L. (1994). Towards an account of causation in a multilingual text generation system. In *Proceedings of the Seventh International Workshop on Natural Language Generation*. https://aclanthology.org/W94-0313.

Denison, D. (1993). *English Historical Syntax: Verbal Constructions*. London: Longman.

De Smet, H. (2012). The course of actualization. *Language*, *88*, 601–633.

De Smet, H. (2013). *Spreading Patterns: Diffusional Change in the English System of Complementation*. Oxford: Oxford University Press.

De Smet, H., D'hoedt, F., Fonteyn, L., & van Goethem, K. (2018). The changing functions of competing forms: Attraction and differentiation. *Cognitive Linguistics*, *29*, 197–234.

Detges, U. (2023). Does reanalysis need ambiguity? In M. Bauer & A. Zirker (Eds.), *Strategies of Ambiguity* (pp. 220–244). New York: Routledge.

Detges, U., & Waltereit, R. (2011). Turn-taking as a trigger for language change. In S. Dessí Schmid, U. Detges, P. Gévaudan, W. Mihatsch, & R. Waltereit (Eds.), *Rahmen de Sprechens. Beiträge zu Valenztheorie und Varietätenlinguistik, Kreolistik, Kognitiver und Historischer Semantik* (pp. 175–189). Tübingen: Narr.

Diessel, H. (2019). *The Grammar Network: How Linguistic Structure is Shaped by Language Use*. Cambridge: Cambridge University Press.

Diessel, H. (2023). *The Constructicon: Taxonomies and Networks*. Cambridge: Cambridge University Press.

Diessel, H., & Hetterle, K. (2011). Causal clauses: A cross-linguistic investigation of their structure, meaning and use. In P. Siemund (Ed.), *Linguistic Universals and Language Variation* (pp. 21–52). Berlin: Mouton de Gruyter.

Ehmer, O., & Rosemeyer, M. (2018). Inferences in interaction and language change. *Open Linguistics*, *4*, 1–20.

Evans, N. (2007). Insubordination and its uses. In I. Nikolaeva (Ed.), *Finiteness: Theoretical and Empirical Foundations* (pp. 366–431). Oxford: Oxford University Press.

Fillmore, C. J. (1982). Frame semantics. In Linguistic Society of Korea (Ed.), *Linguistics in the Morning Calm* (pp. 111–138). Seoul: Linguistic Society of Korea.

Fillmore, C. J., Kay, P., & O'Connor, M. C. (1988). Regularity and idiomaticity in grammatical constructions. *Language, 64*, 501–538.

Fischer, O. (2007). *Morphosyntactic Change: Functional and Formal Perspectives*. Oxford: Oxford University Press.

Fitzmaurice, S., & Smith, J. (2012). Evidence for the history of English: Introduction. In T. Nevalainen & E. C. Traugott (Eds.), *The Oxford Handbook of the History of English* (pp. 19–36). New York: Oxford University Press.

Flach, S. (2020). Constructionalization and the Sorites Paradox. In L. Sommerer & E. Smirnova (Eds.), *Nodes and Networks in Diachronic Construction Grammar* (pp. 45–67). Amsterdam: Benjamins.

Ford, C. E. (1993). *Grammar in Interaction: Adverbial Clauses in American English Conversation*. Cambridge: Cambridge University Press.

Fraser, B. (2006). Towards a theory of discourse markers. In K. Fischer (Ed.), *Approaches to Discourse Particles* (pp. 189–204). Amsterdam: Elsevier.

Fried, M., & Nikiforidou, K. (Eds.). (2025). *The Cambridge Handbook of Construction Grammar*. Cambridge: Cambridge University Press.

Garmonsway, G. (Ed.). (1991). *Ælfric's Colloquy*. New York: Appleton-Century-Crofts.

Gildea, S., & Barðdal, J. (2023). From grammaticalization to Diachronic Construction Grammar: A natural evolution of the paradigm. *Studies in Language, 47*, 743–788.

Gillmann, M. (2024). Allostructions and stancetaking: A corpus study of the German discourse management constructions *wo/wenn wir gerade/schon dabei sind. Cognitive Linguistics, 35*, 67–107.

Gisborne, N. (2008). Dependencies are constructions: A case study in predicative complementation. In G. Trousdale & N. Gisborne (Eds.), *Constructional Approaches to English Grammar* (pp. 219–255). Berlin: Mouton de Gruyter.

Gisborne, N. (2011). Constructions, Word Grammar, and grammaticalization. *Cognitive Linguistics, 22*, 155–182.

Gisborne, N. (2017a). Defaulting to the new Romance synthetic future. In N. Gisborne & A. Hippesley (Eds.), *Defaults in Morphological Theory* (pp. 151–581). Oxford: Oxford University Press.

Gisborne, N. (2017b). Word Grammar morphology. In J. Audring & F. Masini (Eds.), *The Oxford Handbook of Morphological Theory* (pp. 327–345.). Oxford: Oxford University Press.

Givón, T. (1979). *On Understanding Grammar*. New York: Academic Press.

Goldberg, A. E. (1995). *Constructions: A Construction Grammar Approach to Argument Structure.* Chicago: University of Chicago Press.

Goldberg, A. E. (2002). Surface generalizations: An alternative to alternations. *Cognitive Linguistics, 13,* 327–356.

Goldberg, A. E. (2003). Constructions: A new theoretical approach to language. *Trends in Cognitive Sciences, 7,* 219–224.

Goldberg, A. E. (2006). *Constructions at Work: The Nature of Generalization in Language.* Oxford: Oxford University Press.

Goldberg, A. E. (2013). Constructionist approaches. In T. Hoffmann & G. Trousdale (Eds.), *The Oxford Handbook of Construction Grammar* (pp. 15–31). New York: Oxford University Press.

Goldberg, A. E. (2019). *Explain Me This: Creativity, Competition, and the Partial Productivity of Constructions.* Princeton: Princeton University Press.

Goldberg, A. E., & Jackendoff, R. (2004). The English Resultative as a family of constructions. *Language, 80,* 532–568.

Grossman, E., & Noveck, I. (2015). What can historical linguistics and experimental pragmatics offer each other? *Linguistics Vanguard, 1,* 145–153.

Hansen, M.-B. M. (2012). The semantics of pragmatic expressions. In H.-J. Schmid (Ed.), *Cognitive Pragmatics* (pp. 589–613). Berlin: De Gruyter Mouton.

Heine, B., Claudi, U., & Hünnemeyer, F. (1991). *Grammaticalization: A Conceptual Framework.* Chicago: University of Chicago Press.

Higashiizumi, Y. (2006). *From a Subordinate Clause to an Independent Clause: A History of English because-clause and Japanese kara-clause.* Tokyo: Hituz Syobo.

Hilpert, M. (2008). *Germanic Future Constructions: A Usage-based Approach to Language Change.* Amsterdam: Benjamins.

Hilpert, M. (2013). *Constructional Change in English: Developments in Allomorphy, Word-Formation and Syntax.* Cambridge: Cambridge University Press.

Hilpert, M. (2014). *Construction Grammar and its Application to English.* Edinburgh: Edinburgh University Press.

Hilpert, M. (2015). From hand-carved to computer-based: Noun-participle combining and the upward-strengthening hypothesis. *Cognitive Linguistics, 26,* 1–36.

Hilpert, M. (2021). *Ten Lectures on Diachronic Construction Grammar.* Leiden: Brill.

Hilpert, M. (2024). Corpus linguistics meets historical linguistics and construction grammar: How far have we come, and where do we go from here? *Corpus Linguistics and Linguistic Theory*, *20*, 481–504.

Hoffmann, T. (2022). *Construction Grammar: The Structure of English*. Cambridge: Cambridge University Press.

Hollmann, W. B. (2009). Semantic change. In J. Culpeper, F. Katamba, P. Kerswill, R. Wodak, & T. McEnery (Eds.), *English Language: Description, Variation and Context* (2nd ed., pp. 301–313). Basingstoke: Palgrave.

Holmes, J., & Hudson, R. (2006). Constructions in Word Grammar. In J.-O. Östman & M. Fried (Eds.), *Construction Grammar(s): Cognitive Grounding and Theoretical Extensions* (pp. 243–272). Amsterdam: Benjamins.

Hopper, P. J. (2011). Emergent grammar and temporality in interactional linguistics. In P. Auer & S. Pfänder (Eds.), *Constructions: Emerging and Emergent* (pp. 22–44). Berlin: De Gruyter Mouton.

Hopper, P. J., & Traugott, E. C. (2003). *Grammaticalization* (2nd revised ed.). Cambridge: Cambridge University Press.

Hudson, R. A. (1984). *Word Grammar*. Oxford: Blackwell.

Hudson, R. A. (1990). *English Word Grammar*. Oxford: Blackwell.

Hudson, R. A. (1996). *Sociolinguistics* (2nd revised ed.). Cambridge: Cambridge University Press.

Hudson, R. A. (1997a). Inherent variability and linguistic theory. *Cognitive Linguistics*, *8*, 73–108.

Hudson, R. A. (1997b). The rise of auxiliary *do*: Verb-non-raising or category strengthening? *Transactions of the Philological Society*, *95*, 41–72.

Hudson, R. A. (2007). *Language Networks: The New Word Grammar*. Oxford: Oxford University Press.

Hudson, R. A. (2008). Word Grammar and Construction Grammar. In G. Trousdale & N. Gisborne (Eds.), *Constructional Approaches to English Grammar* (pp. 257–302). Berlin: Mouton de Gruyter.

Hudson, R. A. (2010). *An Introduction to Word Grammar*. Cambridge: Cambridge University Press.

Hudson, R. A. (2017). French pronouns in cognition. In N. Gisborne & A. Hippesley (Eds.), *Defaults in Morphological Theory* (pp. 114–50). Oxford: Oxford University Press.

Hundt, M., Mollin, S., & Pfenninger, S. (Eds.). (2017). *The Changing English Language: Psycholinguistic Perspectives*. Cambridge: Cambridge University Press.

Ingham, R. (2012). Anglo-Norman and the 'plural history' of French: The connectives *pourtant* and *à cause que*. *Revue française de linguistique appliquée, XVI*, 107–119.

Israel, M. (1996). The *way* constructions grow. In A. E. Goldberg (Ed.), *Conceptual Structure, Discourse and Language* (pp. 217–230). Stanford: CSLI.

Kanetani, M. (2016). A note on the *Because* X Construction: With special reference to the X-element. *Studies in Language and Literature. [Language]*, *68*, 63–80.

Kapatsinski, V. (2018). *Changing Minds Changing Tools: From Learning Theory to Language Acquisition to Language Change*. Cambridge, MA: MIT Press.

Kemenade, A. van. (1994). Old and Middle English. In E. König & J. van der Auwera (Eds.), *The Germanic Languages* (pp. 110–141). London: Routledge.

Kemmer, S., & Barlow, M. (2000). Introduction: A usage-based conception of language. In M. Barlow & S. Kemmer (Eds.), *Usage-Based Models of Language* (pp. vii–xxviii). Stanford: CSLI.

Kemmer, S., & Verhagen, A. (2005). The grammar of causatives and the conceptual structure of events. *Cognitive Linguistics, 5*, 115–156.

König, E., & Siemund, P. (2000). Causal and concessive clauses: Formal and semantic relations. In E. Couper-Kuhlen & B. Kortmann (Eds.), *Cause, Condition, Concession, Contrast: Cognitive and Discourse Perspectives* (p. 341–360). Berlin: Mouton De Gruyter.

Kortmann, B. (1997). *Adverbial Subordination: A Typology and History of Adverbial Subordination Based on European Languages*. Berlin: Mouton de Gruyter.

Kranich, S., & Breban, T. (Eds.). (2021). *Lost in Change: Causes and Processes in the Loss of Grammatical Elements and Constructions*. Amsterdam: Benjamins.

Kroch, A. S. (1989). Reflexes of grammar in patterns of language change. *Language Variation and Change, 1*, 199–244.

Kroon, C. (1995). *Discourse Particles in Latin: A Study of NAM, ENIM, AUTEM, VERO and AT*. Amsterdam: J.C. Gieben.

Labov, W. (1972). *Sociolinguistic Patterns*. Philadelphia: University of Pennsylvania Press.

Langacker, R. W. (1977). Syntactic reanalysis. In C. N. Li (Ed.), *Mechanisms of Syntactic Change* (pp. 57–139). Austin: University of Texas Press.

Langacker, R. W. (1987). *Foundations of Cognitive Grammar, Volume I: Theoretical Prerequisites*. Stanford: Stanford University Press.

Langacker, R. W. (2008). *Cognitive Grammar: A Basic Introduction*. New York: Oxford University Press.

Lass, R. (2000). Language periodization and the concept 'middle'. In I. Taavitsainen, T. Nevalainen, P. Pahta, & M. Rissanen (Eds.), *Placing Middle English in Context* (pp. 7–42). Berlin: Mouton de Gruyter.

Lenker, U. (2007). *Forhwi* 'because': Shifting deictics in the history of English causal connection. In U. Lenker & A. Meurman-Solin (Eds.), *Connectives in the History of English* (pp. 193–227). Amsterdam: Benjamins.

Levshina, N., Geeraerts, D., & Speelman, D. (2013). Mapping constructional spaces: A contrastive analysis of English and Dutch analytic causatives. *Linguistics, 51*, 825–854.

Los, B., & Komen, E. (2012). Clefts as resolution strategies after the loss of a multifunctional first position. In T. Nevalainen & E. C. Traugott (Eds.), *The Oxford Handbook of the History of English* (pp. 822–834). New York: Oxford University Press.

Lyngfelt, B. (2018). Introduction: Constructicons and constructicography. In B. Lyngfelt, L. Borin, K. Ohara, & T. T. Torrent (Eds.), *Constructicography: Constructicon Development across Languages* (pp. 1–18). Amsterdam: Benjamins.

Meillet, A. (1958 [1912]). L'évolution des formes grammaticales. In *Linguistique historique et linguistique générale* (pp. 130–148). Paris: Champion.

Michaelis, L. A. (2013). Sign-Based Construction Grammar. In T. Hoffmann & G. Trousdale (Eds.), *The Oxford Handbook of Construction Grammar* (pp. 133–152). New York: Oxford University Press.

Milroy, J., & Milroy, L. (1985). Linguistic change, social network and speaker innovation. *Journal of Linguistics, 21*, 339–383.

Mittwoch, A., Huddleston, R., Collins, P., & Pullum, G. K. (2002). The clause: adjuncts. In R. Huddleston & G. K. Pullum (Eds.), *The Cambridge Grammar of the English Language* (pp. 663-784). Cambridge: Cambridge University Press.

Nikiforidou, K., & Fischer, K. (2015). On the interactions of constructions with register and genre. *Constructions and Frames, 7*, 137–149.

Noël, D. (2007). Diachronic construction grammar and grammaticalization theory. *Functions of Language, 14*, 177–202.

Norde, M. (2009). *Degrammaticalization*. Oxford: Oxford University Press.

Perek, F. (2012). Alternation-based generalizations are stored in the mental grammar: Evidence from a sorting task experiment. *Cognitive Linguistics, 23*, 601–635.

Petré, P. (2019). How constructions are born: The role of patterns in the constructionalization of *be going to* INF. In B. Busse & R. Möhlig-Falke (Eds.),

Patterns in Language and Linguistics: New Perspectives on a Ubiquitous Concept (pp. 157–192). Berlin: De Gruyter Mouton.

Quirk, R., Greenbaum, S., Leech, G., & Svartvik, J. (1985). *A Comprehensive Grammar of the English Language*. London: Longman.

Rissanen, M. (2011). On the long history of English adverbial subordinators. In A. Meurman-Solin & U. Lenker (Eds.), *Connectives in Synchrony and Diachrony in European Languages*. Helsinki: Research Unit for Variation, Contact and Change in English. www.helsinki.fi/varieng/journal/volumes/08/rissanen.

Rissanen, M., & Tyrkkö, J. (2013). *The Helsinki Corpus of English Texts (HC)*. https://varieng.helsinki.fi/series/volumes/14/rissanen_tyrkko/.

Rosenbach, A. (2007). Emerging variation: Determiner genitives and noun modifiers in English. *English Language and Linguistics*, *11*, 143–189.

Sag, I. A., Boas, H. C., & Kay, P. (2012). Introducing Sign-Based Construction Grammar. In H. C. Boas & I. A. Sag (Eds.), *Sign-Based Construction Grammar* (pp. 1–29). Stanford: CSLI.

Schiffrin, D. (1987). *Discourse Markers*. Cambridge: Cambridge University Press.

Schmid, H.- J. (Ed.). (2017). *Entrenchment and the Psychology of Language Learning: How We Reorganize and Adapt Linguistic Knowledge*. Berlin: De Gruyter Mouton.

Schmid, H.- J. (2020). *Dynamics of a Linguistic System: Usage, Conventionalization, and Entrenchment*. Oxford: Oxford University Press.

Schmid, H.- J., & Mantlik, A. (2015). Entrenchment in historical corpora? Reconstructing dead authors' minds from their usage profile. *Anglia*, *133*, 583–623.

Schneider, E. W. (2011). *English Around the World: An Introduction*. Cambridge: Cambridge University Press.

Schreier, D., Hundt, M., & Schneider, E. W. (Eds.). (2020). *The Cambridge Handbook of World Englishes*. Cambridge: Cambridge University Press.

Smirnova, E., & Sommerer, L. (2020). The nature of the node and the network: Open questions in Diachronic Construction Grammar. In L. Sommerer & E. Smirnova (Eds.), *Nodes and Networks in Diachronic Construction Grammar* (pp. 1–42). Amsterdam: Benjamins.

Smith, J., & Holmes-Elliott, S. (2022). Tracking linguistic change in childhood: Transmission, incrementation, and vernacular reorganization. *Language*, *98*, 98–122.

Sommerer, L., & Smirnova, E. (Eds.). (2020). *Nodes and Networks in Diachronic Construction Grammar*. Amsterdam: Benjamins.

Sommerer, L., & Van de Velde, F. (2025). Constructional networks. In M. Fried & K. Nikiforidou (Eds.), *The Cambridge Handbook of Construction Grammar* (pp. 220–245). Cambridge: Cambridge University Press.

Steels, L. (2013). Fluid Construction Grammar. In T. Hoffmann & G. Trousdale (Eds.), *The Oxford Handbook of Construction Grammar* (pp. 153–167). New York: Oxford University Press.

Sweetser, E. (1990). *From Etymology to Pragmatics: Metaphorical and Cultural Aspects of Semantic Structure*. Cambridge: Cambridge University Press.

Taylor, J. (2003). *Linguistic Categorization* (3rd. ed.). Oxford: Oxford University Press.

Torrent, T. T. (2015). On the relation between inheritance and change: The constructional convergence and construction network reconfiguration hypotheses. In J. Barðdal, E. Smirnova, L. Sommerer, & S. Gildea (Eds.), *Diachronic Construction Grammar* (pp. 173–211). Amsterdam: Benjamins.

Torres Cacoullos, R., & Walker, J. A. (2009). The present of the English future: Grammatical variation and collocations in discourse. *Language, 85*, 321–354.

Townend, M. (2006). Contact and conflicts: Latin, Norse, and French. In L. Mugglestone (Ed.), *The Oxford History of English* (pp. 61–85). Oxford: Oxford University Press.

Traugott, E. C. (2010). (Inter)subjectivity and (inter)subjectification. In K. Davidse, L. Vandelotte, & H. Cuyckens (Eds.), *Subjectification, Intersubjectification, and Grammatialization* (pp. 29–71). Berlin: De Gruyter Mouton.

Traugott, E. C. (2022). *Discourse Structuring Markers in English: A Historical Constructionalist Perspective on Pragmatics*. Amsterdam: Benjamins.

Traugott, E. C., & Trousdale, G. (2013). *Constructionalization and Constructional Changes*. Oxford: Oxford University Press.

Trousdale, G. (2025). Word formation change in Word Grammar: Two case studies. In E. D. Eppler, N. Gisborne, & A. Rosta (Eds.), *Word Grammar, Cognition and Dependency* (pp. 104–125). Cambridge: Cambridge University Press.

Ungerer, T., & Hartmann, S. (2023). *Constructional Approaches: Past, Present, and Future*. Cambridge: Cambridge University Press.

Van de Velde, F. (2014). Degeneracy: The maintenance of constructional networks. In R. Boogaart, T. Colleman, & G. Rutten (Eds.), *Extending the Scope of Construction Grammar* (pp. 141–179). Berlin: De Gruyter Mouton.

Warner, A. R. (1993). *English Auxiliaries: Structure and History*. Cambridge: Cambridge University Press.

Weinreich, U., Labov, W., & Herzog, M. (2017). Empirical foundations for a theory of language change. In W. Lehmann & Y. Malkiel (Eds.), *Directions for Historical Linguistics* (pp. 95–189). Austin: University of Texas Press.

Wogan-Browne, J. (2009). General introduction: What's in a name: The 'French' of 'England'. In J. Wogan-Browne (Ed.), *Language and Culture in Medieval Britain: The French of England, 1100–1500* (pp. 1–16). Cambridge: Cambridge University Press.

Wolfram, W., Hudley, A. H., & Valdés, G. (Eds.). (2023). *Language and Social Justice in the United States*. Special issue of *Daedalus* 152.

Zwicky, A. (2005). *More illusions*. http://itre.cis.upenn.edu/.

Acknowledgements

We are grateful to many colleagues for discussing the issues outlined in this *Element*. Special thanks for insightful comments and suggestions on an earlier version to Nadine Dietrich, Nikolas Gisborne, Martin Hilpert, Richard Hudson, Yueh-hsin Kuo, Muriel Norde, Eva Zehentner, and an anonymous reviewer. We would also like to thank the series editors and Isabel Collins at Cambridge University Press for their helpful advice and assistance.

Cambridge Elements ☰

Construction Grammar

Thomas Hoffmann
Catholic University of Eichstätt-Ingolstadt

Thomas Hoffmann is Full Professor and Chair of English Language and Linguistics at the Catholic University of Eichstätt-Ingolstadt. His main research interests are usage-based Construction Grammar, language variation and change and linguistic creativity. He has published widely in international journals such as *Cognitive Linguistics*, *English Language and Linguistics*, and *English World-Wide*. His monographs *Preposition Placement in English* (2011) and *English Comparative Correlatives: Diachronic and Synchronic Variation at the Lexicon-Syntax Interface* (2019) were both published by Cambridge University Press. His textbook on *Construction Grammar: The Structure of English* (2022) as well as an Element on *The Cognitive Foundation of Post-colonial Englishes: Construction Grammar as the Cognitive Theory for the Dynamic Model* (2021) have also both been published with Cambridge University Press. He is also co-editor (with Graeme Trousdale) of *The Oxford Handbook of Construction Grammar* (2013, Oxford University Press).

Alexander Bergs
Osnabrück University

Alexander Bergs joined the Institute for English and American Studies at Osnabrück University, Germany, in 2006 when he became Full Professor and Chair of English Language and Linguistics. His research interests include, among others, language variation and change, constructional approaches to language, the role of context in language, the syntax/pragmatics interface, and cognitive poetics. His works include several authored and edited books (*Social Networks and Historical Sociolinguistics*, *Modern Scots*, *Contexts and Constructions*, *Constructions and Language Change*), a short textbook on *Synchronic English Linguistics*, one on *Understanding Language Change* (with Kate Burridge) and the two-volume *Handbook of English Historical Linguistics* (ed. with Laurel Brinton; now available as five-volume paperback) as well as more than fifty papers in high-profile international journals and edited volumes. Alexander Bergs has taught at the Universities of Düsseldorf, Bonn, Santiago de Compostela, Wisconsin-Milwaukee, Catania, Vigo, Thessaloniki, Athens, and Dalian and has organized numerous international workshops and conferences.

About the Series

Construction Grammar is the leading cognitive theory of syntax. The present Elements series will survey its theoretical building blocks, show how Construction Grammar can capture various linguistic phenomena across a wide range of typologically different languages, and identify emerging frontier topics from a theoretical, empirical and applied perspective.

Cambridge Elements ☰

Construction Grammar

Elements in the Series

A full series listing is available at: www.cambridge.org/EICG

For EU product safety concerns, contact us at Calle de José Abascal, 56–1°, 28003 Madrid, Spain or eugpsr@cambridge.org.

www.ingramcontent.com/pod-product-compliance
Ingram Content Group UK Ltd.
Pitfield, Milton Keynes, MK11 3LW, UK
UKHW022139120526
471007UK00012B/1139